CULTURE SMART!
INDIA

Nicki Grihault

·K·U·P·E·R·A·R·D·

First published in Great Britain 2003
by Kuperard, an imprint of Bravo Ltd
59 Hutton Grove, London N12 8DS
Tel: +44 (0) 20 8446 2440 Fax: +44 (0) 20 8446 2441
www.culturesmartguides.com
Inquiries: sales@kuperard.co.uk

Culture Smart! is a registered trademark of Bravo Ltd

Distributed in the United States and Canada
by Random House Distribution Services
1745 Broadway, New York, NY 10019
Tel: +1 (212) 572-2844 Fax: +1 (212) 572-4961
Inquiries: csorders@randomhouse.com

Eighth printing (revised) 2006

Series Editor Geoffrey Chesler

ISBN-13: 978 1 85733 305 3
ISBN-10: 1 85733 305 5

British Library Cataloguing in Publication Data
A CIP catalogue entry for this book is available from the
British Library

Printed in Malaysia

This book is available for special discounts for bulk purchases for
sales promotions or premiums. Special editions, including
personalized covers, excerpts of existing books, and corporate
imprints, can be created in large quantities for special needs.

For more information in the U.S.A. write to Special
Markets/Premium Sales, 1745 Broadway, MD 6–2, New York,
NY 10019 or e-mail specialmarkets@randomhouse.com.

In the United Kingdom contact Kuperard publishers at the
above address.

Cover image: The *nandi* of the Temple, Mysore, Karnataka.
Travel Ink/Simon Reddy

CultureSmart!Consulting and **Culture Smart!** guides have both
contributed to and featured regularly in the weekly travel program
"Fast Track" on BBC World TV.

About the Author

NICKI GRIHAULT is an English travel writer and journalist who has lived and worked abroad for many years, particularly in India. Previously at *Woman Abroad*, she now works as travel editor of *Executive Woman* magazine, and writes on cross-cultural issues for **CultureSmart!**Consulting. She is the author of *Working in Asia* (In Print, 1996).

Other Books in the Series

- Culture Smart! Argentina
- Culture Smart! Australia
- Culture Smart! Belgium
- Culture Smart! Brazil
- Culture Smart! Britain
- Culture Smart! China
- Culture Smart! Costa Rica
- Culture Smart! Cuba
- Culture Smart! Czech Republic
- Culture Smart! Denmark
- Culture Smart! Finland
- Culture Smart! France
- Culture Smart! Germany
- Culture Smart! Greece
- Culture Smart! Hong Kong
- Culture Smart! Hungary
- Culture Smart! Ireland
- Culture Smart! Italy
- Culture Smart! Japan
- Culture Smart! Korea
- Culture Smart! Mexico
- Culture Smart! Morocco
- Culture Smart! Netherlands
- Culture Smart! New Zealand
- Culture Smart! Norway
- Culture Smart! Panama
- Culture Smart! Peru
- Culture Smart! Philippines
- Culture Smart! Poland
- Culture Smart! Portugal
- Culture Smart! Russia
- Culture Smart! Singapore
- Culture Smart! Spain
- Culture Smart! Sweden
- Culture Smart! Switzerland
- Culture Smart! Thailand
- Culture Smart! Turkey
- Culture Smart! Ukraine
- Culture Smart! USA
- Culture Smart! Vietnam

Other titles are in preparation. For more information, contact: info@kuperard.co.uk

The publishers would like to thank **CultureSmart!**Consulting for its help in researching and developing the concept for this series.

contents

contents

Map of India

introduction

*"India is a land of contrasts, of some very rich and
many very poor people, of modernism and
medievalism . . . India is not a poor country. She is
abundantly supplied with everything that makes a
country rich, yet her people are very poor."*
Jawaharlal Nehru

These words are as true today as when Nehru
penned them in 1944. Modern India is a vast
country, full of complexity and contradictions. It
has great natural beauty as well as urban ugliness
wrought by extreme poverty. This paradox can
best be understood by recognizing that India
exists in several centuries at the same time. A
small, sophisticated modern elite of a few million
lives surrounded by hundreds of millions of
primitive people. India has the largest pool of
scientists and technologists after the United
States, yet almost half of its population is
illiterate. It is the birthplace of two major world
religions, yet its temples stand on squalid,
polluted streets. It is a place where monkeys leap
around the shrines, cows weave placidly and in
complete safety among the traffic, and people are
scattered by rickshaws hurtling along the roads.

It is impossible to be unmoved by India. "Visit
India, and you will never be the same again," say
the tourist brochures. It is true. The very name

stirs the imagination, and a visit is an adventure. India will change you.

It is difficult to generalize about Indian culture. India's multilayered peoples have diverse languages, religions, attitudes, and ways of life. Yet from all this emerges an underlying cultural unity that gives rise to a distinctive Indian way of being.

Culture Smart! India sets out to explain India to the foreign visitor. It describes the Indian psyche, attitudes, and values, touching on all aspects of life, from the market place to the boardroom. It gives the first-time visitor a basic cultural orientation, and forms an ideal companion to conventional travel guides. *Culture Smart! India* will not tell you what time a train departs, but it will help you to understand the behavior of the people on it.

The Indians you will meet may or may not have certain expectations of Westerners. Whatever the case, they will appreciate politeness, patience, gentleness, and an understanding of what makes up the many facets of their lives. Whether you are going to India on business or for pleasure, an awareness of the background, customs, and way of life of what was once the "jewel in the Crown" of the British Empire, and is now described as "an awakening giant" will enable you to have an enlightening, fruitful, and rewarding visit.

culture smart! india

Key Facts

Official Name	The Republic of India	In Hindi, *Bharat.*
Capital City	New Delhi	Population 9,421,000
Main Cities	Major ports are Mumbai (Bombay), the largest city, with over nine million people, Kolkata (Calcutta), and Chennai (Madras).	Other large cities are Bangalore, Hyderabad, Ahmadabad, Kanpur, Pune, Nagpur, Bhopal, Jaipur, Lucknow, and Surat.
Area	1,269,219 sq. miles (3,287,263 sq. km.)	India is the seventh largest country in the world.
Climate	Varies from tropical monsoon in the south to temperate in the north.	
	June–October: heavy summer monsoon rains arrive from the SW. December–February: northerly winds reduce rainfall, bringing drought till March–May.	
	In the mountains temperatures vary with altitude and rainfall is more evenly distributed.	
	On the northern plains, rainfall decreases E–W, with desert conditions in the far W.	
	On the central Deccan plateau temperatures vary with altitude: it is tropical in the S with high humidity. The W coast is rainy throughout the year. The SE coast is subject to cyclones and storms, with high temps. and humidity during the monsoon period.	

Land Use	Arable land 56%; permanent crops 1%; permanent pastures 4%; forests and woodland 23%; other16%.	
	Most Indians are farmers. The best agricultural land is in the E, subject to flood control measures. Rice is cultivated on the coastal plains, sugarcane in the Punjab, and coffee in Coorg on the Western Ghats.	
	India is the world's largest tea producer, the third-largest producer of milk and tobacco, and the fourth-largest producer of wheat, coal, and nitrogenous fertilizers.	
Currency	The Rupee, abbreviated as Rs. At the time of writing, U.S. $1 = 46.540 rupees; £1 = 70 rupees.	The rupee is made up of 100 *paise*. One *lakh* is the term for 100,000 rupees, and one *crore* for 10 million rupees.
Population	1,029,991,145 (July 2001, est.)	The world's second-most populous country.
Ethnic Makeup	Very diverse. 72% of Indo-European descent; 25% Dravidian (mostly in the south), 3% Mongoloid.	
Age Structure	0–14 years 33.12% 15–64 years 62.2% 65 years and over 4.68%	
Religion	Hindus (83%); Muslims 11%); Sikhs (2%); Christians (2.5%); Parsis, Jains, and Buddhists (1.5%).	

Key Facts

Languages	The official language is Hindi, written in the Devanagri script. Most people, especially in the cities, know some English.
	17 other official languages: Assamese, Bengali, Gujarati, Kannada, Kashmiri, Konkani, Malayalam, Manipuri, Marathi, Nepali, Oriya, Punjabi, Sanskrit, Sindhi, Tamil, Telugu, Urdu. There are more than 1,650 dialects.
Government	The world's largest democracy—a liberal democratic federal republic within the Commonwealth. The seat of government is in the capital, New Delhi. The president, elected for a five-year term, appoints a prime minister. There are two houses of Parliament, the upper Council of States (*Rajya Sabha*) and the House of the People (*Lok Sabha*).
	There are 28 states and 7 centrally administered Union Territories. Each state has an Assembly, and a governor appointed by the president.
Media	All India Radio (AIR) is the national service run by the Ministry of Information and Broadcasting. Its home service covers 24 languages and 146 dialects. TV programs are in Hindi or the language of the area; many English programs are from America. Commercial stations include satellite and cable.

Media: English Language	Major English-language newspapers include *The Times of India*, *The Hindu*, *The Statesman*, *The Indian Express*, *India World*, *The Economic Times*, *The Financial Express*. Many regional papers, such as *The Deccan Herald*, *The Maharashtra Herald*.	
Electricity	220 volts AC, 50 cycles generally. Some areas also have DC supplies. Light sockets are the bayonet type; plugs 15 amp and 5 amp with three round pins.	Check the voltage before using appliances. Socket sizes vary, so take a set of plug adaptors; American appliances will not operate without a transformer.
Video/TV	The British PAL system is used.	
Telephone	India's country code is 91.	To dial out of India dial 00, folllowed by the country code.
Opening Hours: Banks	10:00 a.m. – 2:00 p.m. Mondays to Fridays, 10:00 a.m. – 12:00 noon Saturdays.	
Opening Hours: Post Offices	10:00 a.m. – 5:00 p.m. Mondays to Fridays. Saturdays, morning only.	
Red Tape	All visitors need a visa. Tourist visas, obtainable from embassies or consulates, are normally valid for ninety days from the date of issue.	
Time Difference	GMT + 5.5 hours (winter); GMT + 4.5 hours (summer).	

LAND &
PEOPLE

THE INDIAN SUBCONTINENT

The Republic of India *(Bharat)* constitutes much
of the greater portion of the Indian subcontinent.
It is a huge and varied country,
rimmed by the beautiful, snow-
capped Himalayan mountains
in the north, with ninety-five
peaks above 24,600 feet
(7,500 meters), and
extending 2,000 miles into
the Indian Ocean in the
south. In between lies every
imaginable landscape, from fertile plains, drained
by the major Ganges and Indus Rivers, to the
central Deccan plateau bounded by the mountain
ranges of the Eastern and Western Ghats, to the
tropical rainforest of Kerala in the far south; the
Thar desert in the northwest covers an enormous
area almost twice the size of Bangladesh.

The seventh-largest country in the world, India
is as large as the whole of Europe and more
diverse, and around one-third the size of the

United States. The distance between the oil fields in the Gujarati plains in the west and the tea gardens of Assam in the northeast is 1,700 miles, which gives some idea of its extent.

India is bounded by Pakistan and the Arabian Sea on the west, and Bangladesh, Myanmar (Burma), and the Bay of Bengal in the east. To the north lie China, Nepal, and Bhutan, and the sea separates India from Sri Lanka in the south. Although it is on a main trading route and has absorbed many peoples and influences over the centuries, India's position, and its configuration as a subcontinent, is important in that this has helped it to remain apart from the rest of Asia. This isolation has led to the development of a rich and distinct cultural identity.

CLIMATE

Because India is so vast, temperatures vary immensely. April, May, June, and July are generally very hot except in the hill stations on the foothills of the Himalayas. The average temperature in New Delhi, for instance, ranges from 45°F to 70°F (7°C to 21°C) in the cool months to 75°F to 106°F (26°C to 41°C) in the heat of summer. Darjeeling, on the lower slopes of the Himalayas, in the east, has a near-tropical climate in summer, and is chilly from November to March, and some of the hill stations have snow in winter. The southwest monsoon, when it doesn't fail, lashes the west coast and the windward slopes of the Western Ghats. Avoid it from June to August. The wettest place on earth is Mawsynram in the northeast, where 467.5 inches (11,873mm) of rain fall each year—ten times more than in New York, and twenty times more than in London.

The best time to visit most of India is from October to March, between the hot season and the monsoon. India is, nevertheless, considered a year-round destination because conditions vary on both a seasonal and a regional basis. The trick is to be in the right place at the right time.

WHAT WILL THE WEATHER BE LIKE?	
December, January, February	cool months
March, April, May	hot summer months
June, July, August	southwest monsoon
October, November	northeast monsoon

THE PEOPLE

India is heir to one of the world's oldest and most advanced civilizations. The ancient Indians made notable intellectual contributions and laid the foundations for geometry, arithmetic, and algebra.

Modern India has about a billion people and is one of the most ethnically diverse places in the world. Its distinctive culture has arisen through the absorption of numerous waves of migrating peoples who swept into the country over several thousand years. Even now, you can see distinct ethnic groups, the pale, green-eyed Aryan stock contrasting with those of Mongolian origin in the north and the dark-skinned, dark-eyed people of the south. Tall Sikhs tower over the usually smaller Indian frame.

Despite extensive birth control programs, a baby is born every 1.2 seconds in India. With its population growing at an annual rate of 3 percent, India is on its way to becoming the most populated country in the world by 2050. It is also one of the world's poorest nations, with half the population in a state of poverty.

Seventy-two percent of the population live in rural areas; the 28 percent who live in the cities are now equivalent to the entire population at the time of independence in 1947. The cities attract a constant flow of migrants from the countryside.

A third of the population is to be found in the vast, fertile Indo-Gangetic plain that unfolds at the foot of the Himalayas, and stretches from the Punjab in the west to Bengal in the east. India's capital city, New Delhi, is located in this region.

SOME FAMOUS INDIANS

Mohandas Karamchand Gandhi (1869–1948)
Perhaps the best-known Indian statesman in the West. He led India's independence movement and was renamed *Mahatma* ("Great Soul") Gandhi because he spent some fifty years of his life helping the poor of India, especially the so-called "untouchables." He urged that the road to independence be achieved through nonviolent means.

Siddartha Buddha (c.563–483 BCE)
Founder of the Buddhist religion.

Jawaharlal Nehru (1889–1964)
India's first Prime Minister.

Indira Gandhi (1917–84)
India's first female Prime Minister. No relation to the Mahatma, but the daughter of Nehru. Unusually for the time she married a Parsi, named Gandhi.

Jiddu Krishnamurthi (1895–1986)
Leading Indian mystic.

Rabindranath Tagore (1861–1941)
Bengali poet and Nobel Laureate who founded a school (Shantiniketan, "abode of peace") famous for its progressive ideas.

B. K. S. Iyengar (1918–)
Founder of a major yoga method.

Rich and Poor

There are roughly 300 million middle-class consumers in India with near-European spending power. About the same number live, or try to stay alive, below any humanly accepted poverty line. Those in between may earn a reasonable living, or get by somehow. A tiny proportion of the population is phenomenally wealthy, and many of these belong to the princely classes. Even at the height of the British Raj only three-fifths of India was under direct British rule. More than half a million square miles were fairly autonomous states ruled by Maharajas (great kings) and Nawabs (Muslim ruling princes). After their privy purses were abolished by Prime Minister Indira Gandhi, some of the autonomous state rulers went into business and turned their palaces into hotels. The Lake Palace Hotel at Udaipur, made famous in the James Bond film *Octopussy*, is a good example.

India's Cows

Cows and bullocks are an essential part of the rural economy: they pull plows, help irrigate fields, and draw carts to market. Cows supply some milk (although very poor yields by Western standards). There are over 400 million cows in India—about one cow for every two people. In Hindu belief the cow is considered holy, therefore no one dares kill one. Fodder, however, is so scarce in many parts of the country that cows find their way into the towns (helped on their way by the owners!) where they are allowed to wander around at will, grazing where they can.

THE STATES OF INDIA		
State	**Capital**	**Location**
Andhra Pradesh	Hyderabad	Central southeast
Arunachal Pradesh	Itanagar	Far northeast
Assam	Dispur	Northeast
Bihar	Patna	Northeast, with the hill station of Darjeeeling
Chhattisgarh	Raipur	Central east
Goa	Panaji	Southwest
Gujarat	Gandhinagar	West
Haryana	Chandigarh	North central
Himachal Pradesh	Shimla	North central; houses the Tibetan Buddhist enclave of Dharamsala
Jammu & Kashmir	Srinagar	Far northwest
Jharkhand	Ranchi	Northeast; formerly southern Bihar
Karnataka (formerly Mysore)	Bangalore	Southwest
Kerala	Trivandrum	Far southwest, also home to Cochin
Madhya Pradesh	Bhopal	Center
Maharashtra	Mumbai	Central southwest
Manipur	Imphal	Far northeast
Meghalaya	Shillong	Northeast
Mizoram	Aizawl	Far northeast
Nagaland	Kohima	Far northeast
Orissa	Bhubaneshwar	East
Punjab	Chandigarh	Northwest

State	Capital	Location
Rajasthan	Jaipur	Northwest
Sikkim	Gangtok	Northeast
Tamil Nadu	Chennai (Madras)	Far southeast
Tripura	Agartala	Far northeast
Uttaranchal	Dehra Dun	Northeast; formerly northern part of Uttar Pradesh
Uttar Pradesh	Lucknow	Central northeast; contains the cities of Agra and Varanasi
West Bengal	Calcutta	Northeast

UNION TERRITORIES AND SPECIAL AREAS

Andaman & Nicobar Islands	Port Blair	Bay of Bengal, south of Burma
Chandigarh	Chandigarh	Northwest
Dadra & Nagar Haveli	Silvassa	West
Daman & Diu	Daman	West
Delhi (gained National Capital Territory status in 1991)	Delhi	North central
Lakshadweep, Minicoy & Amindivi Islands	Kavaratti	Arabian Sea, off Malabar Coast
Pondicherry	Pondicherry	Far southeast

CITY FLAVORS

The first thing that strikes
visitors on arriving in
India is the teeming,
overcrowded streets
in cities that never
seem to sleep. Indian
cities are all full of
crowds, smells, noise,
and color, but each has its
own distinctive flavor.

Delhi's bustling old city is very poor, but rich in
historic architecture, and has a traditional Indian
atmosphere. The capital city of New Delhi is
another world, laid out by the English in the early
twentieth century. Broad avenues with grand state
buildings lead to boutiques and burger bars
frequented by the middle classes.

Kolkata (Calcutta), in Bengal, has an
international reputation for squalor and
poverty. However, it is also known as "the soul
of India" for its intellectual and political activity.
It is also a major manufacturing, commercial,
shipping, and metalwork center. The Bengali
people are known for their friendliness. Calcutta
attracts many migrants from Bangladesh.

Mumbai (Bombay), capital of Maharashtra, is
the most cosmopolitan of India's cities. It
handles a third of the country's foreign trade

and has a large financial center at Nariman Point. The rich live next to squalid slums.

Chennai (Madras), in Tamil Nadu, is the least westernized of the big cities of India. Tamil Nadu has less foreign influence, and a more traditional way of life. Facilities are poor here.

Other large cities of interest include **Hyderabad,** in Andra Pradesh, famous for its handicrafts; **Bangalore,** in Karnataka, known as the "silicon valley" of India; **Ahmadabad,** in Gujarat, which has sumptuous brocades; **Pune,** notable for the large Rajneesh ashram; the leather manufacturing city of **Kanpur** in Uttar Pradesh; **Surat** in Gujarat, famous for its silk prints; **Jaipur,** called the pink city, after the color of the stone used to build the palaces; **Amritsar,** the holy city of the Sikhs, famous for the Golden Temple; and the holy city of **Varanasi** (Benares), so-called because of its many temples and its location on the banks of the sacred River Ganges.

INDIA: A BRIEF HISTORY

The origins of Indian civilization lie in the Indus Valley, where a highly developed urban culture was well established in Harappa, Mohenjo-daro, and Lothal by 2500 BCE. Archaeological remains point to large houses with broad streets and good drainage systems, and include artistically engraved soapstone seals. We don't know who these ancient people were, or what language they spoke. It is generally accepted, though, that five of the six major ethnic groups that make up the population of India today were already in place when the Indo-European Aryans arrived from Central Asia around 1500 BCE.

The Aryans brought with them the four *Vedas* (Sanskrit for "knowledge"), ancient Sanskrit hymns and devotional formulae that have been preserved by the Hindu tradition—first orally and then in written form. Much of our knowledge of this period of Indian history comes from the two great Indian epics, the *Mahabharata* and the *Ramayana*.

The terms "Hindu" and "Hinduism" were coined by nations outside India to designate the people and religion of the country to the east of the river Sindhu, or Indus. Ironically, the River Indus, after which India is named, is now mainly in Pakistan.

From the fourth century BCE to the thirteenth century CE, the Indian subcontinent was united and ruled by a series of empires, the most famous of which was the empire of Ashoka, who presided over the expansion of Buddhism in India. You can still find stone inscriptions to Ashoka in different parts of the country. The central symbol of the Indian national flag is the Ashoka Wheel.

The last great empire was that of the Guptas, but under weak rulers the Gupta empire disintegrated into regional states, which allowed

Turko-Afghan rulers to establish a Muslim sultanate in the north, with Delhi as its capital. At this time India's ruling class embraced both Hindus and Muslims. Under the Delhi sultanate a land revenue system was developed that resulted in revolts by the large peasant landowners. India was then invaded by the Mongol leader Timur (Tamerlane), whose descendants founded the Mogul Empire. The Moguls are remembered in India for their magnificent buildings—the Taj Mahal was built by the Mogul ruler Shah Jahan—and their beautiful miniature paintings.

Less well known is the fact that they created India's first national administration, which extended from the northwest to Bengal in the east, and from the Himalayas to Konkan in the south. The administrators, known as *mansabs,* came from the noble class, and organized production and trade between the states. India was an agricultural country, and the diversion of up to 50 percent of the produce into trade and tribute led to protest and revolt by the peasantry that in turn weakened the central empire in the seventeenth and eighteenth centuries. By the eighteenth century India had broken up into regional empires such as Bengal, Awadh, Maharashtra, Hyderabad, and the Punjab.

Many Hindus believe that the coming of the Muslim rulers in 1206 made it easier for the Europeans to establish a foothold in the subcontinent. The fabled riches of the East drew European traders. The Portuguese came to Goa in 1510 and stayed until 1961. As one would expect, five centuries of Portuguese influence has made Goa very different from the other Indian states. Many of the people speak Portuguese.

Then, in 1600, Queen Elizabeth I of England granted a charter to the East India Company, heralding the arrival of the British in India. At first the British were traders like the other European nationalities. When the British community in Bengal under Robert Clive ("Clive of India") antagonized its ruler, Siraj-al-Daulah, he ransacked their settlement and imprisoned the captives in what became known as the "Black Hole of Calcutta." The result was the battle of Plassey in 1757, after which the British established themselves as rulers in Bengal, from where they proceeded to expand across India.

British rule was imposed by the East India Company, a commercial body under the statutory control of the government in London. Under Clive, British administration, law and order, education, and the Church of England were introduced. From 1772 to 1785 Warren Hastings, the governor-general of Bengal, raised a native army and pursued expansionist policies.

One of the last of the colonial powers to leave India was France. The Compagnie des Indes was set up in Pondicherry, about a hundred miles south of Madras, in 1674. After almost a hundred years of rivalry, scheming, and outright warfare, the British finally defeated the French in 1761. However, the story did not end there. Pondicherry was given back to France, and was not finally ceded to the Indian Republic until 1954. Even today it has a distinctly French character.

"The Jewel in the Crown"

British East India Company rule ended in 1857 with the outbreak of the Indian Mutiny, a widespread uprising led by sepoys (Indian soldiers serving in the British Bengal Army). After a year of reconquest the British government decided to rule India directly as the greatest of its colonies. In 1877 Queen Victoria was crowned Empress of India—the "jewel" in the Imperial Crown.

Imperial rule was a mixture of paternalism and racism, and already in 1885 the Indian National Congress was founded in Bombay to militate against the more repressive aspects of the British *Raj*—the Hindi word for "rule." However it was not until a lawyer, Mohandas Karamchand ("Mahatma") Gandhi, succeeded in uniting the property-owning and business classes into a united National Congress Party that real opposition to the British was established.

Gandhi's unique approach was to use non-violence as a means of opposition. He wrote: "I contemplate a mental and therefore moral opposition to immoralities. I seek entirely to blunt the edge of the tyrant's sword, not by putting up against it a sharper-edged weapon but by disappointing his expectation that I should be offering physical resistance."

Gandhi's passive resistance campaign culminated in independence from Britain in 1947, but against his wishes India was partitioned into two separate states—India and Pakistan. Pakistan became a Muslim state, ruled by the Muslim League under Muhammad Ali Jinnah. The partition was marked by much bloodshed and mass migration, and tension between the two countries continues to exist to this day.

Pakistan itself was divided into two parts. The Punjabi power center in West Pakistan was physically separated by northern India from the more populous Bengali province of East Pakistan. In 1971, East Pakistan, aided by India, seceded from West Pakistan to form the independent country of Bangladesh.

The Influence of the British Raj

The British were largely responsible for developing the great port cities of Calcutta, Bombay, and Madras. The foundations of Calcutta were laid in 1690, which greatly influenced its present infrastructure. The British created a network of roads, canals, and railways, and introduced their own legal system and procedures. An education system was developed for "imparting to the native population knowledge of English literature and science through the medium of the English language."

At the time of the British arrival, India had a strong mercantile capitalist economy. Britain, however, restructured the economy to serve her own imperial interests, disrupting much of the indigenous infrastructure and impeding the development of India's own culture. The Indian Civil Service is also a legacy of the Raj. Over the years this has mushroomed into a large, unwieldy bureaucracy that has become a perfect vehicle for red tape and corruption.

Unlike the Portuguese, who became integrated into the life of Goa, the British remained aloof from their subject peoples. In many subtle ways, this served to undermine the indigenous culture and language. They maintained an elitist lifestyle, considering their own culture and religion to be so superior as to give them a mandate to govern.

Wanting To Be British

During my time as a teacher in India, I asked my class what they most wanted to be when they grew up. "I want to be English," replied a six-year-old girl.

Venika Kingsland

Cultural imperialism has created other problems in India. For example, on the one hand there is a growing Hindu fundamentalist backlash against the advance of secular Western values, and on the other the desire to emigrate to Britain, where there is "equality of opportunity" for all, is greater than ever. There is a huge difference between the younger generation of Indians, who may have lived and worked overseas, and their fathers and uncles who have not had the opportunity to travel.

Although the British Raj came to an end in 1947, when India gained her independence, it has left a lasting influence. The British colonial tradition is evident in architecture, government, and sport, and Victorian values are still alive and well in the Golf and Gymkhana Clubs in the metropolitan cities of India. Many Indians who feel "British" are in a time warp, and assume the values and customs of the Raj—which in England today are considered quite strange.

India Since 1947

Immigration to Britain, and increasingly now to the United States, has been a major feature of life for India's trading and urban working classes. Their places in the larger Indian cities have been taken by country dwellers who migrate to the cities in huge numbers in times of drought. It is important to understand that, despite its traditionalism, India's instincts are liberal and socialist. It is also important to recognize that the population and size of India make it difficult to control. The huge influx from the countryside into the cities makes them almost ungovernable. To arrive in the city and to live in one of the vast shanty towns that surround it is for the great majority their future. To break out of the shanties is almost unheard of.

If Gandhi was the father of the nation founded at midnight on August 14, 1947 (hence the title of Salman Rushdie's novel *Midnight's Children*), the natural first Prime Minister was his close associate, the brilliant Jawaharlal Nehru. Under Nehru, India, while remaining within the British Commonwealth, became part of the Non-Aligned group in the United Nations. He committed himself to trying to alleviate India's poverty and to abolishing the caste system.

Gandhi died in 1948, shot by a Hindu fundamentalist, leaving Nehru totally in charge.

Some Key Dates

c.2500 BCE – Indus Valley civilization flourishes.

c.1500 BCE – Aryan invaders conquer northern India and the Deccan plateau. Brahminic caste system developed.

326 BCE – Alexander the Great enters northwest India.

321–184 BCE – The Mauryan dynasty first to unify the subcontinent.

262 BCE – The Mauryan Emperor Ashoka converts to Buddhism; unifies most of India except for the far south; establishes Buddhism as the state religion.

320–480 CE – Gupta dynasty reunifies northern India. Golden age of Hindu literature, art, and science.

480–90 – Raids by the White Huns from Central Asia plunge India into anarchy.

7th–8th centuries CE – Muslim influence grows.

11th–12th centuries – Raids by Turks, Arabs, and Afghans.

1206 – First Muslim sultanate established in Delhi.

1398 – The Mongol Timur (Tamerlane) sacks Delhi.

1498 – First Portuguese traders arrive in Calicut, followed by French, Dutch, and British.

1510 – Portuguese capture Goa.

1526 – Timur's descendant Babur occupies Delhi. Founds the Mogul dynasty.

1562 – Emperor Akbar marries a Hindu princess. Extends pan-Indian Mogul Empire. Consolidated by Aurangzeb.

14th–16th centuries – The Hindu south remains independent under the Vijayanagar dynasty.

1600 – Elizabeth I grants Charter to the East India Company. Trading posts and settlements follow in Surat, Madras, Bombay, and Calcutta.

1672 – French settle Pondicherry.

1756-63 – The Seven Years' War between France and Britain.

1760 – British East India Company the effective ruler of India following the battle of Plassey in 1757.

1857 – The Indian Mutiny. Uprising against British rule, crushed by 1858.

1858 – Government transferred from the East India Company to the British Crown. India formally incorporated into the British Empire. Late 19th-century movement for independence.

1885 – India National Congress founded; a rallying point for national feeling.

1919 – British forces kill 379 Indian demonstrators at Amritsar. Government of India Act; elected Indian ministers share power with appointed British governors.

1920s onward – Mahatma Gandhi's civil disobedience and passive resistance campaigns.

1935 – Further Act allows election of provincial governments.

1947 – India gains independence from Britain and is divided into the dominions of India (predominantly Hindu) and Pakistan (predominantly Muslim).

1948 – Gandhi assassinated by a Hindu fanatic.

1950– India becomes a Republic within the Commonwealth.

In 1950 India declared itself a Republic with Nehru as Head of State and Prime Minister. After his death in 1964, Nehru was succeeded as Prime Minister by his daughter, Indira Gandhi, in 1966, reflecting the huge respect in which professional women are held in India. In 1984 she was assassinated by her Sikh bodyguards, and was succeeded by her second son, Rajiv. He was assassinated by Tamil Tiger guerrillas during the election campaign of 1991, and although the Congress Party swept into power on a sympathy vote, deprived of the charismatic Gandhi leadership it was unable to maintain its hold on the popular imagination. The death of Rajiv Gandhi ended the unbroken dominance of the "Nehru dynasty," although his Italian-born widow, Sonia, remained active in Indian politics.

India then came under the governance of the Janata Dal party. The secular Janata Dal was supported by the Bharatiya Janata Party (BJP), which is the party of fundamentalist Hinduism. Over the next ten years the BJP became the most powerful party in India and formed the government. Despite fears that the emergence of militant Hinduism was a threat to other groups, the BJP broadened its power base by promoting liberal economic reforms.

INDIA TODAY

In 1947 Jawaharlal Nehru spoke of India's tryst with destiny. More than fifty years later, India remains a nation of contrasts. Although it is economically self-sustaining and a net exporter of grain, 46 percent of its adult citizens remain illiterate. Its "silicon valley," Infosys Park, outside Bangalore, generates $4 billion a year and expands at 50 percent a year, but more than one-third of the world's poor live in India, which ranks 134th of the 174 countries on the UNDP's development index. India is a nuclear power and has produced its own supersonic fighter aircraft, but its cities are overcrowded and chaotic, with no primary health care, pure drinking water, or sanitation.

The roots of this imbalance lie in the regulated socialist economy that was put in place by Nehru. This was broken up only in 1991 to release entrepreneurial talent and in response to pressure from a rising population that by 2050 will overtake that of China. Finally, the secular state that Nehru envisaged and tried to build is in danger of being overtaken by Hindu nationalism on the one hand and Muslim extremism on the other.

On the cultural side, India leaps ahead with some of the world's most famous novelists, most popular films, and most exciting scientific discoveries. In the twenty-first century India has a long way to go.

Political Flashpoints

Over the last few years India has maintained her Non-Aligned status while developing nuclear potential. She has fought three wars with Pakistan since independence. A key political issue remains the dispute over the mainly Muslim state of Kashmir. This is a subject to be avoided. There are also border problems with China.

Although Indians have largely learned to live in harmony, religious or communal riots and civil unrest do break out from time to time. The rise of Hindu fundamentalism in recent years has led to violence between Hindus and Muslims. Election time, therefore, is not the time to be in India.

It is best to avoid talking politics in India, although the Indians themselves enjoy such discussions. As an outsider, you are best advised to remain in the role of listener.

GOVERNMENT AND POLITICS

Despite the existence of more than a hundred different ethnic subgroups within the country, India has remained a cohesive democracy since independence in 1947. It is the world's largest democracy and a multiparty federal Republic. The head of the Republic is the President, elected every five years by parliament, but the real power lies in the hands of the head of government, the Prime Minister. The country is divided politically into twenty-eight states and seven union territories. Each state, and Delhi, has its own elected governor and ministers.

The national parliament in Delhi consists of two multiparty legislative houses. The upper house is the Council of States, *Rajya Sabha,* with 250 members. The lower house is the *Lok Sabha,* which has 545 members. The main political parties in India are the Congress Party, successor to Gandhi's Indian National Congress (a cross-caste and cross-religion coalition, left of center), the Janata Dal, or People's Party (secular, left of center) and the Bharatiya Janata Party, or BJP (radical right-wing Hindu nationalist party). From Independence until 1996 Congress was the dominant party. In 1996 the BJP had its first brief spell in government, and in 1999

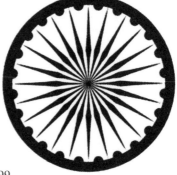

became the largest party in parliament, presiding over a growing economy and opening up negotiations with Pakistan over Kashmir. In the general elections of 2004, Congress, headed by Sonia Gandhi, surprised the pundits by becoming once more the largest party in the country. In a further dramatic twist, she declined to take office as prime minister of the future Congress-led coalition.

VALUES &
ATTITUDES

What Indians Believe In:	Key Indian Values:	What Indians Hate:
Fatalism/*karma*	Respect for tradition	Loss of face
Strength of family and professional group	Compromise	Personal criticism
Human warmth	Respect for elders	Being patronized
Gentleness	Creativity	Impiety
Tradition	Eloquence	Bad *karma*
	Asceticism	Being rushed
	Democracy	
	Reincarnation	

India is an ancient civilization, and its people have a predominantly religious attitude to life, marked by clear authority structures and distinct social status lines. This is not to suggest that the Indians are not "go-ahead" and able to break through the system. For example, the Prime Minister, a high-caste Brahmin, is committed to breaking down caste differences, and one of his actions has been to appoint a Dalit, an "untouchable," as president of the BJP. Nevertheless, there are certain values and attitudes that enable Indians who live in extreme poverty to understand and accept their lot in life, even if it is not easy to bear.

THE LIFE CYCLE, *KARMA*, AND REINCARNATION

Indians tend to worry less than Westerners about missed opportunities, as they believe that what goes around will come around again, perhaps in a different guise. Their fundamental belief is in the continuity of life, and the Western notion of "seizing the day" is less current in India than "going with the flow."

The cause of this attitude is the very deep-seated belief in *karma* (Sanskrit, "fate"). *Karma* is the belief that what you do in this life will affect you in subsequent lives. If you have a bad situation in this life, then it may be because of something you did in a previous existence. *Karma* may be good or bad. If I am successful it is good *karma*; if I have bad fortune it is bad *karma*. I may do what I can to enhance the influence of good *karma* or mitigate the influence of bad *karma*, but ultimately everything that happens in my life is my *karma* and must be accepted with equanimity.

Alongside the belief in *karma* is the belief in

reincarnation. Traditional Indian belief says that we have been born many times and will be born many times more. When we die we are reincarnated according to our *karma*, what we have done in our previous life. Life on earth is intended to improve our spiritual state by doing well with the good things we have, or working through the harmful things we have done in previous incarnations. Therefore beggars subsisting in hovels in the center of town are not a national scandal: it's just *karma*. The *begum* in her stately palace is not socially irresponsible. It's her *karma*. If you believe in improvement over many lifetimes, it certainly means you take a long view.

An old proverb sets out the pattern of Indian life. When you are young you grow up and have a family; then you make money to keep your family and yourself in good health. When you are old you stop making money and work to attain wisdom and improve your *karma* for your next life.

FAMILY STRENGTH

The Indians take great strength from their families, which are larger and more extended than those in most Western countries. It is significant that while Western families are declining, Indian families are increasing in size. The Indian diaspora is as big as the Chinese. An Indian computer programmer living in London or Seattle may have family in Birmingham, England, in Canada, in Kansas, and in Turkey as well as in India in Bangalore and in villages outside. Young children from families in the village may work in their better-off relatives' houses in the city.

Poorly educated men and women may work in support roles in the head of the family's enterprise. What we see as nepotism, or even exploitation, many successful Indians see as the exercise of familial responsibility.

Families are a source both of great strength and of great demands. In India, as in Africa, the need to be responsive to and responsible for families can be a drain on both time and resources.

THE TRADE GROUP

A key strength for the Indian community is the trade group. The closest European equivalent to the Indian trade group is the guilds. The Indian trade group is at one level a spin-off from the social grouping epitomized by the caste system. It combines not just standards of professionalism and commitment but also closure to outsiders and mutual support. Arranged marriages are common between members of a trade group and are used to strengthen relations within the group. Also, if a member of a trade group is in difficulties, then other members will rally round with organizational and financial help. Good examples of trade groups are the traditional textile and diamond industries.

One of the outcomes of the existence of trade groups is that when you contact an Indian businessperson, it is unlikely that you will deal with a single individual. That first contact may just be with someone who is deemed to be good at communication with foreigners. Behind him, or her, may be a whole range of other individuals providing support in finance, strategy, product control, etc., not all working for the same firm but all cooperating by virtue of their common trade group affiliation.

The close relationship of family and trade group also helps to explain why business centers of excellence are often regionally based: Mumbai (Bombay) is a commercial and media center, and Bangalore is an IT center, although at least one Indian commentator has attributed its IT explosion to the mathematical orientation of the Dravidian mind (the Dravidians are the native peoples of Bangalore). It is generally accepted that they are very good at math—especially the Brahmins.

WARMTH AND GENTLENESS

Although extremely pragmatic in business and sometimes quite violent in public demonstration, the Indians personally are taught to cultivate a spirit of warmth and gentleness to others. Part of this comes from the belief in *karma* and reincarnation, but it is also part of the reciprocal relationship between authority and obedience. Within a company framework, in return for obedience and contribution to the owner's wealth, the owner is expected to be humane and to further the promotion of subordinates. In India you do not ask for promotion. You expect it to come when you are ready for it. In a family business the eldest son is expected to take over the business, and is groomed for it. The father owes him the duty of a good education. In return, the son owes his father the duty of studying hard.

Looking only at the commercial operation, an outsider may not see the relationships behind the scenes. What the Westerner may see as sweatshop exploitation of, for example, nine-year-old children sewing the seams of soccer balls, the Indian owner may see as giving an opportunity to work and earn money.

However, there is another side to this. In India, business success automatically brings increased status, and the Indians are pragmatic risk-takers. They take a positive attitude toward innovation, but the drive to get results means that honesty is not a major value. As Richard Lewis points out in his book *When Cultures Collide,* stealing crops may be as honorable as growing them, and highwaymen have their own trade group! This is simply seen as a double standard by the West, and is a source of confusion and sometimes distrust.

For Indians there is no problem with profit. It means security, success, and status. Success is *karma.* Lack of profit is seen with the same detached eye. Failure is also *karma.* Maybe next time, in another life, perhaps.

RESPECT FOR TRADITION

Another source of confusion for Westerners is the Indian ability to respect tradition while being bold in experimentation. India is the land of the nuclear bomb, of some of the finest IT specialists in the world, and of real, live, sacred cows. These worlds coexist without undue stress. Alongside the business gurus are the Sadhus, or holy men. Alongside the air conditioning and the skyscrapers are the traditional village structures. Alongside aspiration and getting ahead is caste.

An important part of India's tradition is respect for elders. As in all of Asia, this is manifested in the treatment of older family members or company members, regardless of seniority.

ASCETICISM

An interesting feature of Indian life is the lack of decoration and apparent care in many Indian dwellings, compared to those in the West, and the opulence and ostentation of others. India, even when it can afford it, is not the land of the house and garden makeover that is modern America and Britain. Nor is it the place where you will find dull exteriors masking superbly beautiful courtyards and interiors, as in Spain or Latin America. It is unwise to generalize, but Indians admire the simple life and the purity of the soul, and do not necessarily feel that outward trappings are important. It helps to explain why dirt and the sensual bombardment of sights, sounds, colors, and smells—a cacophony of the senses—that many Western visitors to India at first find so upsetting, don't disturb most Indians. It also explains why they accept, to a degree, the manifestation of extreme poverty in every area of life in the streets. It is as much a mistake to confuse asceticism with estheticism as it is to confuse estheticism with morality.

COLOR AND CREATIVITY

In fact, the incredible, almost gaudy atmosphere of so much of Indian daily life and celebration is at one level the exuberance of a deep well of creativity; this expresses itself in the musicals of Bollywood, the decorations of the temples, and the advertising in towns. It is also evident in the way people talk— colorful, florid, inventive language, in love with images and experimentation.

In technology, the Indians have an amazing do-it-yourself creativity that has enabled them to find solutions to many problems. India and Indians can assault the visitor with an overabundance of food, drink, talk, wealth, crowds, and decoration. In India it is very easy to feel you are losing control, and old "India hands" will tell you that there is only one way to regain that control—to dive in and swim.

TIME

Time for the Indians is not an issue. They expect to put relationships first, and to spend time building them. They are concerned with knowing what type of person they are dealing with. If they invite you home they are looking to see how you behave, how you respond to them, whether you are good with children, whether you respect their cultural values.

They may expect to invest a week with you, to take you up into the mountains, and show you their country, and will be disappointed but not necessarily surprised when you tell them you can give them two days. Time invested, lots of it and over a long period, invariably pays off in India. Time rationed usually doesn't.

DEMOCRACY

What surprises people about India, despite its patriarchal and traditional values, is its passion for democracy. This comes from two sources: the social ideas of Mahatma Gandhi himself and, above all, the determination of Jawaharlal Nehru to create a country of "400 million

people capable of governing themselves."
Nehru's state-planned officially regulated
economy has failed, but up to now his vision of
democracy has succeeded.

THE INDIAN PSYCHE

Indian culture is family-oriented and
patriarchal. This strongly religious society has
great respect for age, tradition,
and sacred symbols. People
dress and present
themselves modestly,
and don't tolerate
behavior contrary to
religious tradition.
The key impact of religion
on daily life is through the
inequality posed by the caste

system, and the accompanying belief in *karma,*
or fate (which exonerates bad driving on the
buses, for example). A wide chasm exists
between rich and poor, and social mobility is
difficult if not impossible. The caste system
means accepting one's place, even by living on
the street, and accounts for the acceptance of a
large beggar class. However, people are not
expected to show emotion in the face of their
fate, and assertiveness is the norm.

The Indians are proud of their country. They believe in simple material comforts and rich spiritual accomplishments. The nurturing of relationships, tolerance, social harmony, and hospitality are paramount. People do things through friends and relatives, so approach anything you need to get done with this in mind. Privacy is not important here. India is a collectivist culture. Ideals of humility and self-denial are respected.

The ability to absorb many different cultural influences and integrate them into their own religious and philosophical framework is an Indian trait. Their bureaucracy is perhaps an unfortunate example of this. Where you might expect forms to be filled out in triplicate, in India, they must be filled out ten times.

Three aspects of life you're assured of during a visit to India are slowness, delays, and lots of paperwork. Waiting in long lines is a fact of life, and punctuality is not an Indian quality. These small daily trials will give you the chance to develop your own qualities of patience, tolerance, and understanding, and perhaps to discover your limits!

Although it is tempting to romanticize India and its people, there are practices such as bride burning and female infanticide that should not be forgotten (see Marriage, in

Chapter 4). For these and other reasons life can be cheap here, and religious beliefs assist with the acceptance of its fragility.

> **Don't Talk Loudly and Don't Talk Down**
> *"'Pushy,' 'aggressive,' and 'loud' are considered bad words in our vocabulary. They show a lack of breeding. Talking down is the worst insult you can deliver to an Indian."*
> **Vinita, an Indian living in the United States**

ATTITUDES TOWARD FOREIGNERS

India has been much invaded and exploited over the centuries—by Mongols, Muslims, the French, and the British, and economically, they feel, by the Americans. From each historical experience India has learned, but a residual suspicion remains. It is very important for Indians, in whatever walk of life, to feel that their culture is respected, and foreigners should take care not to cause loss of face by giving personal criticism.

What the Indians have learned is that bridging the cultural gap between Westerners and Easterners is not difficult; indeed, most Indians manage it with more ease and sophistication than most Westerners.

The Indian people are friendly, polite, and very interested in foreigners, especially the British, for the memory of the Raj still commands respect, and a surprising lack of malice. Courtesy and hospitality to foreigners are ingrained, and you will probably be surprised and touched by acts of hospitality and kindness that cross religious boundaries.

People feel it is only polite to make conversation with you in public places. In about ten minutes they know all about you—your name, job, salary, home, whether you are married, if not, why not, and so on. This can be daunting to the more reticent foreigner.

chapter three

INDIA'S RELIGIONS

India has given the world two of its great religions: Hinduism and Buddhism. Apart from these, several other religions are practiced, and by and large these have happily coexisted in a pluralistic society. Although the Republic has no official religion, and all have equal status, the sheer number of Hindus (83 percent) means that Hinduism is dominant. This guide is therefore biased toward Hindu customs, although mention of those relating to other groups is made wherever appropriate. Other religions include Muslims (11 percent), Christians (2.5 percent), Sikhs (2 percent) and Buddhists (less than 1 percent), Jains (less than 1 percent, but a powerful force), Parsis, and Baha'is.

Taboos are attached to all religions in India, but it is especially important to be aware of the sacredness of the cow and the avoidance of cowhide products (such as shoes and bags) among Hindus. Muslims have a taboo regarding pork and pigskin products. Sikhs and Parsis don't smoke tobacco.

HINDUISM

Hinduism is an important religion not merely by virtue of its many followers, estimated at more than 800 million, but because of its profound influence on various other religions during its long, unbroken history. It is also characterized by not having a founder. There is an extraordinary tendency in Hinduism to absorb foreign elements, and these have contributed to the religion's syncretism—the wide variety of beliefs and practices that it encompasses. As no one can be a Hindu except by birth, the incorporation of older and other religions was perhaps a practical way of increasing the numbers of Hindus. Hindu communities can now be found around the world.

Hinduism embraces many apparent contradictions. These include external observances, and their rejection; extreme polytheism and high monotheism; animal worship, animal sacrifice, and the refusal to take any form of life. All of these, plus the profusion of images adorning the temples, combine to make it difficult for Westerners to understand the underlying unity of Hinduism.

The Real Name for Hinduism

The Hindus themselves do not generally speak of "Hinduism," which is a term used by outsiders for their religious beliefs and practices. They use the term *Sanatana dharma*—the eternal way of life—distinguishing it from Brahmanism or Vedic *dharma*, which is essentially monotheistic, and that part of the religion that has come from the early Indo-European times. Modern Hinduism, as practiced today, probably goes back only a thousand years.

Brahmanism

The word "Brahmanism" pertains to Brahman— the absolute or ultimate reality in Hinduism—and should not be confused with Brahmin, a man of the Brahmin caste (one of the four hereditary castes), or Brahma, the creator god of the Hindu trinity.

Actively promoted at the time, presumably to stem the popularity of other religions such as Buddhism, Islam, and Christianity, a form of devotional Hinduism known as the Bhakti movement started to become popular around a thousand years ago.

The Vedic scriptures, brought by the Indo-European Aryans, and composed in a language similar to old Persian, are the authoritative basis for Hinduism. A central belief is the existence of a cosmic or natural order, a balanced way of living—physically, socially, ethically, and spiritually. The Vedic home is where sunlight and fire were greatly valued, and society was sustained by high ethics and culture. Science was a central concern and technology pursued. Interestingly, the Indo-European Hittites, who arrived in Anatolia via the Caucasus around 2000 BCE, also showed these qualities and the earliest known references to the Vedic gods are found in their inscriptions.

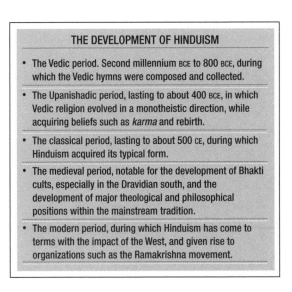

THE DEVELOPMENT OF HINDUISM

- The Vedic period. Second millennium BCE to 800 BCE, during which the Vedic hymns were composed and collected.

- The Upanishadic period, lasting to about 400 BCE, in which Vedic religion evolved in a monotheistic direction, while acquiring beliefs such as *karma* and rebirth.

- The classical period, lasting to about 500 CE, during which Hinduism acquired its typical form.

- The medieval period, notable for the development of Bhakti cults, especially in the Dravidian south, and the development of major theological and philosophical positions within the mainstream tradition.

- The modern period, during which Hinduism has come to terms with the impact of the West, and given rise to organizations such as the Ramakrishna movement.

The Hindu Epics

The two great Hindu epics, the *Ramayana* and the *Mahabharata,* contain inspired moral and ethical teachings. The *Ramayana,* composed by the poet Valmiki in the fifth or sixth century BCE, celebrates the birth, education, and adventures of Rama, the ideal man and king, and his ideal wife, Sita. The surviving text runs to 24,000 couplets. The *Mahabharata:* the great epic of the Bharata Dynasty, relates the struggle between two families, the Kauravas and the Pandavas. It also incorporates a mass of other romantic, legendary, philosophic, and religious material from the heroic days of early Hinduism.

Traditionally ascribed to the sage Vyasa, it was probably the result of two thousand years of shaping before it reached its present written form in around 500 CE. Included in it is the discourse between Krishna and Arjuna, *the Bhagavad Gita: The Lord's Song,* probably Hinduism's most important single text. The *Mahabharata* is made up of 100,000 couplets (making it seven times as long as *The Odyssey* and *The Iliad* combined).

The televised version of these two epics, eighty or ninety episodes each, was viewed by over 100 million viewers in India, irrespective of religion.

Hindu Belief

Hindus believe in one God: Brahman the
Supreme, the ultimate ineffable reality. Their rich
imagination has given concrete form to different
aspects of the mind, and the many faces of reality
are depicted by a wealth of imagery. For example,
the *Trimurti* (the threefold manifestations)
symbolizes three aspects of Brahman. Brahma is
the creator and the first member of the trinity;
Vishnu is the preserver or sustainer; and Shiva the
completer or destroyer. The gods go through the
same experiences as humans on earth, and so
people can relate to them.

Hindus generally fall into three broad groups
of adherents. The first is the *Vaishnavites*, the
followers of Vishnu and of Krishna, who is an
incarnation of Vishnu. The second consists of the
Shaivites, the followers of Shiva. The *Shakti* cults
form the third group and are devotees of the
mother goddess. *Babas* and *gurus* (venerated holy
men) wander through the streets.

Sva-dharma (personal duty) is all-important in
the Hindu faith. The *Bhagavad Gita* makes it clear
that it is better to do one's own duty, however
poorly, than someone else's, however well.

In the Brahmanical system, there are three
stages in life, known as *varnashrams*. These stages
are: *Brahamchari*, the student stage; *Grihastha*,
the householder stage; and *Vanaprastha*, the stage

of one who has retired from active life but continues in a mentoring role. Today, this stage would be known by the politically correct term "the third age." A fourth stage, that of *Sannyasi,* one who has renounced worldly things, was added at a later period, presumably influenced by Buddhism. These stages are observed notionally by all Hindus, but in reality by very few.

Each individual is said to have three obligations: to the gods, addressed through daily worship, rituals and regular guidance provided by priests; to the sages, achieved by the study of the *Vedas,* the chanting of mantras, and through offering hospitality to Brahmins and priests; and to the ancestors, fulfilled by producing a son to perpetuate the family and necessary to perform the funeral rites for ancestors.

HINDUISM'S FOUR ACCOMPLISHMENTS

Hinduism stresses the importance of four human accomplishments. These are:

Artha: acceptance of wealth, possession, and power, the creation of a sustainable society.

Dharma: cosmic order, which is maintained by righteousness and observing social and religious law.

Kama: achieving quality and enjoyment of life in a balanced way, not to be confused with hedonism.

Moksh: the ultimate goal, liberation from the cycle of birth and death.

The Hindus pray in *mandirs,* or temples, which are found everywhere. Although the inner sanctums in many temples are off-limits to non-Hindus, some temples will allow foreigners to go inside, but shoes must be left outside in every case. There is usually someone who will look after them for a couple of rupees.

Some animals, such as monkeys, snakes, bulls, elephants, and eagles, are revered in the Hindu faith. Temples to Hanuman, the monkey god, are to be found in every city, town and Hindu village. Hanuman's wisdom and strength make him the patron god of Indian wrestlers. Every Tuesday morning and lunchtime long lines stretch out in front of one of the famous temples in New Delhi, as office workers come to say their prayers on Hanuman's day. It is therefore also considered auspicious to offer sweetmeats and fruits to live monkeys as they wander in their hordes near temples and in the old parts of cities.

The temple of Karni Devi, together with her mount, a rat, can be found near Bikaner, in Rajasthan. There are literally thousands of rats running everywhere, and one has to be careful. Treading on a rat can be expensive—if a white or black rat is hurt you are obliged to offer its weight in gold or silver!

The Caste System

One of the most talked-about and least understood elements of traditional Indian society is the caste system, which affects politics, business, and social relations. The caste system has evolved over thousands of years as a powerful way of organizing and administering an enormous mass of people. Although discrimination according to caste is now illegal, it still affects who gets what jobs and privileges, and whom people associate with in daily life.

Hindu society is divided into four main castes: Brahmins, Kshatriyas, Vaishyas, and Sudras. Subcastes and extra castes further complicate the social structure. Traditionally, the four castes are said to have been produced by Brahma from different parts of his body at the time when the *Vedas* were revealed to the Brahmins. As an integral part of Indian life, however, the caste system has penetrated other communities; for example, one sometimes hears of Brahmin Catholics.

The first three classes are believed to have originated in the tripartite division of ancient Indo-European society, as seen in Greece and Rome. The Sudras, or servants, were later added as a fourth group when the Indo-Europeans entered the Punjab and began to move down into the Ganges Valley. The fifth group, roughly 15 percent of the population, consists of the outcasts, or "untouchables," who do all the dirty jobs, such as cleaning and refuse disposal. The politically correct term for them is Scheduled Castes, although Mahatma Gandhi gave them the name of Harijan, or "God's people."

Finally, there are the Hijiras, of whom there are approximately a million, living in organized groups all over India. This is the only non-hereditary group, and is comprised of transsexuals, asexuals, transvestites, eunuchs, and so on, from every religion and caste. Hijiras are described in both the *Ramayana* and the *Mahabharata;* eunuchs were also used to guard the women's quarters in the Mogul period. Hijiras make a living by singing, dancing, and making lewd jokes at weddings and other ceremonies such as the birth of a son. They are at once hated, feared, and respected. To be cursed by a Hijira brings bad luck, but a blessing could give you a much-wanted son and heir!

Understanding *Dharma* and *Karma*
The belief in *dharma* (the obligation to accept one's condition and perform the duties appropriate to it) and *karma* (the law of

consequence, or fate) is intrinsic to the whole principle of caste. According to *karma*, every action has a consequence that will come to fruition in either this or a future life. *Karma* governs *samsara* (the cycle of rebirth), in which individuals are reincarnated on earth according to past behavior. Their present situation is the consequence of past actions; by being *dharmic*, that is, obedient to the rules of their caste in this life, they have a chance to be reborn into a higher caste in the future.

Karma therefore discourages people from attempting to cross caste lines for social relations of any kind. No one can escape the obligations of *dharma*, which have to be fulfilled without envy if poor, and without self-criticism if rich. Fortunately, this is breaking down, especially with the younger generation and in the cities.

The belief that behaving in a *dharmic* way will bring about favorable circumstances naturally gives the higher castes the license to behave in any way they like. It enables them to ignore the plight of the poor and accept bribery and corruption as a way of life. This should provide an insight to those visitors who are often at a loss to understand how the extremes of wealth and poverty, animal worship and total animal neglect and abuse, can exist side by side.

Members of a higher caste often assume privileges such as expecting instant service in shops, going to the front of a line, and so on. They are usually recognized only by the way they dress and by their superior attitude toward others around them. Certain Brahmin priests are recognizable through a *bindi* or *tilak* marked on their forehead, depending on the temple or group they are attached to.

Tantra

Tantrism is a current of esoteric thought running parallel with the orthodox Vedic tradition. It emphasizes the feminine aspect of reality; its practitioners aim to unite the universal male-female polarities and so attain freedom *(moksh)*. The purpose of life is to embrace the whole of life itself, and it is by responsible experimentation with life that the individual embraces reality as a whole rather than suffer from the delusion fostered by partial knowledge. Tantric practice uses the body as a vehicle for gaining enlightenment, and includes Mantra and Kundalini yoga.

Entering an Ashram

Because there is a considerable emphasis on personal religion in Hinduism, a multitude of ashrams (religious centers for study and meditation), where holy men teach small groups, are dotted throughout the country. Many of these also offer yoga as an essential element of spiritual practice. Indian spirituality has long fascinated Westerners wishing to broaden their own spiritual experience. Most ashrams are happy for Westerners to visit, and welcome them with customary Indian hospitality.

OTHER RELIGIONS OF INDIA

Islam

In India, 11 percent of the population (over 75 million people) are followers of Islam, which constitutes the largest religious minority in the country. Islam is one of the world's most widespread religions, embraced by a fifth of the world's population. It is not just a personal religion but a complete way of life. The parts of India that came under Muslim rule were profoundly influenced by it and this can clearly be seen in architecture, food, and art.

Founded in Arabia in c. 622 CE, Islam is based on the teachings of the Prophet Muhammad. In middle life he received the call to proclaim the worship of the One God (Allah), against the prevailing polytheism and idol worship of his native Mecca. The Arabic word "Islam" means "entering into a state of peace and security with God through allegiance or surrender to him."

Belief in the absolute, all-encompassing nature of God is the cornerstone of Islam. However, while Allah is the creator of everything, individuals are free to make moral choices, and are judged by their actions.

The uncorrupted word of God, revealed to the Prophet Muhammad, recited by him, and later written down, is recorded in the Koran *(Quran)*, which provides a clearly defined code to live by. The account of "the words, deeds, or silent approval" of the Prophet and his Companions, whose lives were a living commentary on the Koran, is contained in the *Hadith* ("traditions"), the second-most important source of Islamic teaching. Interpretations of the scriptures, applying them to daily life, are contained in codes of religious law, or *Sharia.* The fundamental articles of faith and action that shape Muslim life are expressed in the Five Pillars of Islam.

THE FIVE PILLARS OF ISLAM

Shahada: profession of faith or belief in the Oneness of God and the finality of the prophethood of Muhammad.

Salat: formal prayers that are performed five times a day, which are a direct link between the worshiper and God. There is no hierarchical authority in Islam, and there are no priests. Prayers are led by a learned person who knows the Koran and is generally chosen by the congregation.

Zakat: concern for and almsgiving to the needy. An important principle of Islam is that everything belongs to God, and that wealth is therefore held by human beings in trust. The word *zakat* means both "purification" and "growth." Our possessions are purified by setting aside a proportion for those in need, and for society in general.

Sawm: self-purification through fasting. Every year in the month of Ramadan, all Muslims fast from dawn until sundown, abstaining from food, drink, and sexual relations. Ramadan ends with a feasting festival.

Hajj or Pilgrimage: the pilgrimage to the ancient shrine of the Ka'aba, at Mecca, is an obligation for those who are physically and financially able to make it. It is the culmination of a Muslim's spiritual life, and many will save for years to take the pilgrimage. Every year, over two million people go to Mecca from all over the world.

On Friday, the holy day, special prayers are offered at the mosque. The meat Muslims eat must have been ritually slaughtered *(halal)*. They consider certain animals, such as pigs, dogs, and amphibians, as unclean. They therefore do not eat these animals or use any products made from them. They should not drink alcohol.

Hospitality is an important tenet of the Islamic tradition. Anyone who appears at a meal time, regardless of who they are, is invited to share the meal. Open-heartedness, closeness, and understanding of others are encouraged, and family unity is important.

When visiting mosques, remove your shoes as a mark of respect. You can carry them under your arm. Women must wear a headscarf.

Buddhism

Buddhism first began in India in the sixth century BCE, although today it is better known outside the country. Its founder, Siddhartha Gautama (born c. 624 BCE), was the princely son of the Hindu ruler of the Sakya clan, on the northern edge of the Ganges basin. When he was  twenty-nine he left his life of privilege to try to resolve the problems of existence by embracing extreme ascetic practices. After failing to find peace and a solution to the problem of universal suffering by these means, he reverted to "the middle way" of meditation, and sat beneath a tree to see things as they really are. At the age of thirty-five, after passing through four stages of progressive insight, he experienced enlightenment. He preached that the only escape from suffering lay in the complete renunciation of the world and its pleasures, and by following the right path. He continued traveling around north India and teaching, with a growing band of disciples, until his death at the age of eighty.

The spread of Buddhism through India was accelerated in the third century CE by the Emperor Ashoka. He adapted the social ethic of Buddhism and is regarded by Buddhists as the model of a just ruler. His policies are recorded in carved edicts. By the thirteenth century, however, Buddhism had virtually died out in India under pressure from Hinduism and Islam, except for a few surviving pockets in the northeast.

At the time, the Buddha's teachings were regarded as heretical by the Brahmin Hindu priests because they dispensed with belief in a supreme creator god, and with priestly rites and functions, and disregarded caste differences. Buddhism holds that all phenomena are impermanent and unsatisfactory, and lack a permanent essence, such as a soul. All beings share these characteristics, but can achieve freedom through enlightenment. The self is not permanent, as it is subject to change and decay, and its attachment to impermanent things causes delusion and all kinds of suffering. The path to enlightenment lies in actions that lead to selflessness. A central tenet of Buddhism, which it shares with Hinduism, is the moral law of *karma*, by which good or evil deeds result in reward or punishment in this life, or a succession of rebirths. Hindus consider Buddha to be an incarnation of Vishnu.

The Buddha recognized the source of suffering in the Four Noble Truths, and showed the way of liberation from it through the Eightfold Path. The seeker's goal is *nirvana*, the "blowing out" of the fires of all desires, and the absorption of the self into the infinite.

There are two main traditions within Buddhism, Mahayana and Theravada, encompassing many different schools across Asia. Vajrayana—"thunderbolt" or "diamond-vehicle"—Buddhism is the type practiced in India, as well as in Tibet, Nepal, Bhutan, and Mongolia. Its followers see it as a swift path to enlightenment in this life.

Walk Clockwise Around a Temple

It is traditional to walk clockwise around Buddhist structures, both inside and out. Do not smoke or drink alcoholic beverages while on any hallowed ground, be restrained when taking photographs, and make sure you wear appropriate clothing.

Sikhism

The year 1999 marked the tercentenary of the occasion when the visual symbols of Sikhism, such as uncut hair and the wearing of the turban, were prescribed. This annual festival is known as "Vaisakhi," and is celebrated in April. It commemorates one of the most important events in Sikh history, the institution by Gobind Singh of the *khalsa,* or community of Sikh initiates. Sikhism is one of the world's major religions, with over 20 million followers, most of whom live in the northwest Indian state of Punjab.

Sikhism is a progressive religion, founded by *Guru* (teacher, spiritual guide) Nanak, who was born in 1469. Nanak was a mystic who believed that God can be found within oneself, and transcends religious distinctions. He drew upon what he considered were the best elements of devotional Hinduism and Sufi Islam at the time to formulate the tenets of Sikhism.

Sikhs believe in the absolute unity and sovereignty of God, and reject the idea of a human incarnation. They accept *karma* and *samsara,* and believe that the way to break the cycle is to align one's life with the will of God. They reject rituals and practices like fasting, pilgrimage, omens, and austerities, and stress qualities such as honesty, courage, compassion, generosity, patience, and humility in daily life. Sikhs see themselves as having a modern and practical religion, and they value family life as a good foundation from which to face life's challenges. They must not eat meat slaughtered in a cruel manner; they must abstain from tobacco and alcohol; and they must not commit adultery. All Sikhs are expected to bring about their own personal development, achieved by passing through four stages.

FOUR STAGES OF PERSONAL DEVELOPMENT

Manmukh: a person who is unconsciously incompetent, self centered, and selfish.

Sikh: a person who is trying to learn and develop, and who becomes conscious of his or her own incompetence.

Khalsa: a person who has achieved a measure of selflessness, and is at the stage of conscious competence.

Gurmukh: the ultimate stage, where an individual has developed an inner authority and is able to teach others.

After Guru Nanak came a line of teachers, the tenth being Guru Gobind Singh, born in 1666. At the age of nine, he succeeded his father, Guru Tegh Bahadur, who was beheaded by the Mogul Emperor Aurangzeb. Guru Gobind Singh inherited the responsibility of guiding the Sikhs through troubled times. He not only accomplished this, but went a long way toward fulfilling Guru Nanak's teaching. He managed to eradicate distinctions among his followers on the basis of gender, class, and occupation, and promoted equality of opportunity.

Together with his followers he fought many battles to protect and maintain the Sikh way of life, even enduring the pain of knowing that his two sons were bricked up alive into a wall. In 1708, as he lay dying from his injuries, he declared that there should be no further human gurus. Instead, the Sikh holy scriptures, known as the *Guru Granth Sahib,* should become the teaching. The *Guru Granth Sahib* is a compilation of the thoughts and teachings of all the Sikh gurus and contains 5,867 hymns, as well as compositions by Hindu and Muslim saints. The third and final edition was completed in 1708, and is formally installed in the Golden Temple in Amritsar.

The greatest achievement of Guru Gobind Singh was the creation of the ceremony, on Vaisakhi day in 1699, by which a person becomes *khalsa* (pure). Echoing the original event, the ceremony involves drinking *amrit* (nectar, made from sugar stirred into water with a dagger), in the presence of five *khalsa* Sikhs and the holy scriptures. Following the ceremony, the men are given the title of Singh (lion) and the women that of Kaur (princess).

Guru Gobind Singh gave the Sikhs their most enduring and distinguishing characteristics as a way of differentiating themselves. These physical signs act as a reminder of their purpose in life:

SIKH SYMBOLS

Kesh: long, unshorn hair. A symbol of spirituality, and a reminder to behave like a Guru. Sikh men are expected to wear a turban as a symbol of royalty and dignity. The turban must not be covered by any other headgear, as nothing must come between it and the direct source of knowledge. The turban is mandatory for Sikh men and optional for Sikh women.

Kangha: comb. This represents hygiene and discipline, as opposed to the matted, unkempt hair of ascetics.

Kara: steel bracelet. A symbol of strength and continuity, and a reminder to the wearer to exercise restraint.

Kachha: underpants, which signify self-control and chastity.

Kirpan: ceremonial sword. This is a symbol of dignity and of the historic Sikh struggle against injustice. It is worn purely as a religious symbol, not as a weapon.

Shoes are not allowed into Sikh temples, known as *gurdwaras,* and you should cover your head as a mark of respect.

Jainism

The Jains are a monastic organization, founded by the Hindu monk Vardhamana (c. 549–477 BCE). He became known as Mahavira (Great Hero), and was roughly contemporary with Buddha. Jains believe in the attainment of *nirvana* in life, not after death, by following a set of principles of faith, cognition, and conduct.

The most important principle of Jainism, and one which had a deep influence on Mahatma Gandhi, is *ahimsa,* the avoidance of injury to any living creature. The Jains abhor violence and are strict vegetarians. The orthodox among them wear gauze masks to avoid the accidental inhalation of insects.

Zoroastrianism

Zoroastrianism, which is followed by the Parsis, is one of the oldest religions in the world. It was founded by the prophet Zoroaster, or Zarathustra, in northeastern Iran, in about 1200 BCE. Inspired by a vision of God, the Wise Lord, Ahura Mazda, he taught a form of religion that stressed moral choices and personal responsibility. Under Cyrus the Great his teachings became the official state religion of the Persian Empire in the sixth century CE, holding sway from north India to Greece and Egypt. The *Zend-Avesta* are the sacred scriptures of the faith. The Parsis, who came to India as refugees from Persia, settled mainly in Mumbai (Bombay) and Gujarat.

Fire, symbolizing the sacred fire brought from heaven by Zoroaster, is the central physical representation of belief, and is said to illuminate the mind and purify the spirit. Symbolic fires are kept burning in temples, where the Parsis worship. Truth, and goodness and charity toward others, govern their way of life. The Parsis are a small but important minority, as they form a significant part of the commercial classes. In the days of the British Raj, they adapted quickly to English ways, and were often employed in British companies. They are usually very westernized.

Christianity

The gospel of Christianity was spread in India by St. Thomas—one of the original apostles—who was buried in Madras, making India home to one of the oldest Christian communities in the world. Goa and Kerala are strongholds of the Christian faith. The "incorrupt body" of St. Francis Xavier is kept in a glass coffin in Goa. Brought out every ten years, it draws Christian pilgrims from all over the world.

HOLIDAYS AND FESTIVALS

With seven major faiths, a large agricultural population, and a rich historical and political background, there are many important events and colorful days of celebration throughout the Indian year. In addition, the Indians celebrate changes of season, such as the coming of spring, the monsoon, and harvest time. Festivals also provide occasions for the extended family to come together, and so help to maintain family solidarity.

The main secular national holidays are fixed according to the Gregorian calendar, but older lunar and solar calendars are used in calculating the dates of other festivals, and these can vary slightly from year to year.

Different states may celebrate different religious festivals, and even where the same festival is celebrated across a number of states, its form and traditions can vary according to the community. It is well worth finding out when local festivals take place and sampling those you can for the sheer spectacle.

Remember, though, that many festivals are the occasion for public holidays, so do not to try to do business during festival time. If you are in India on business, it is always a good idea to telephone first before visiting government offices.

NATIONAL HOLIDAYS (fixed dates)

26 January – Republic Day	
1 May – Labor Day	
15 August – Independence Day	
2 October – Mahatma Gandhi's Birthday	
25 December – Christmas Day	

Republic Day marks the day in 1950 when India became a republic and the Constitution of India came into effect. The event is celebrated in each state capital, but most impressively in Delhi, where there is a parade by the Indian army, navy, and air force, followed by floats representing the different parts of the country. Many national awards are made for science, the arts, and social work, and there is a bravery award for children. At the end, the combined bands of the armed forces beat a retreat. The event is televised.

India's Independence Day is the occasion of the Prime Minister's address to the nation, delivered from Delhi's splendid Red Fort, a former Mogul palace. The Lahore Gate of the Red Fort was the place where, at midnight on August 14, 1947, the Union flag of the British Empire was hauled down and the Indian flag raised.

Christmas Day in India is celebrated with the exchange of presents and the singing of hymns in Indian languages, particularly in Goa, Mumbai (Bombay), and Tamil Nadu.

THE FESTIVE YEAR
Apart from these fixed-date holidays, there is a wealth of religious and regional festivals—mainly, but not exclusively, Hindu—that take place at

different times of the year. The dates change according to the lunar year or seasonal cycle. Let us follow them chronologically.

January

There are several harvest festivals in January. In north India the *Lohri* festival celebrates the sugarcane harvest with music, song, and the giving of sweets made of sugar and sesame seeds. In southern India, where rice is the staple, the harvest festival is called *Pongal*. In the *Mattu Pongal* ceremony cattle and cars and tractors are washed and garlanded to honor them for their hard work in bringing in the harvest. In Assam, in the northeast, the harvest festival is called *Bihu*, and elsewhere *Makar Sankranti*.

February-March

The middle or end of February sees a celebration of the god Shiva in *Sivaratri*, in the form of a night of fasting, prayers, and worship with flowers.

There are two early spring festivals. *Vasant Panchami* is celebrated in honor of *vasanta*, or spring, and of Sarasvati, the goddess of learning. The "carnival of riots," *Holi*, takes place at the vernal equinox, on the eve of which huge bonfires are lit. Children and adults celebrate with colored powders and paint.

March-April

Between March and April there are celebrations of the birth of the mythical hero Rama (an incarnation of the Hindu god Vishnu), and of the Jain founder Mahavira.

Vaisakhi is a Hindu spring festival, celebrated with *melas* (fairs), dances, and folk songs. It is of special religious significance to the Sikhs, who celebrate it on or near April 13.

Pooram is a ceremony at Trichur in Kerala. At the time of the flowering of the laburnum, gulmohar, and cassia trees, the temple elephants are brought out for a procession, garlanded, shaded by umbrellas, and accompanied by music, dance, and fireworks.

May-June

Buddha Purnima celebrates the birth, enlightenment, and death of the Buddha.

Before the coming of the monsoon, Indians bathe in the holy River Ganges (now generally known as the Ganga), or in other rivers, and the coming of the rains is celebrated with more music and dance.

In the festival of *Teej*, in honor of Parvati, wife of the god Shiva, married women return to their family homes to get together with their female friends from their premarriage days.

By now the heat is becoming unbearable, and

in the *Rath* festival at Puri, in Orissa, thousands of people pull carts carrying effigies of the local gods to their summer residence.

July-August
In the north of India brothers and sisters celebrate their relationship in the ceremony of *Rakhi Bandhan.* Sisters tie plain or fancy bracelets made of thread around their brothers' wrists as a symbol of protection, loyalty, and affection, and brothers give money or other gifts to their sisters in return. Special friends may also be included in this gift giving, which represents brotherly and sisterly affection.

Janam Ashtami is a nationwide festival in honor of the god Krishna. The celebrations include songs, dances, and plays reenacting his exploits. At night, Hindus bathe and decorate statues of Krishna with basil, and sometimes with dolls and toys for his pleasure.

In Maharashtra (capital, Mumbai, or Bombay) *Ganesh Chaturthi* is a celebration in honor of Ganesh, the elephant-headed god of wisdom and of removing obstacles. Clay images are made that are carried and then immersed in rivers or in the sea, accompanied by dancing and drumming. New ventures, journeys, or celebrations in India begin with a ceremony of propitiation to Ganesh.

Onam (see below) can be celebrated as early as late August.

September-October

To celebrate the end of the monsoon, Kerala celebrates *Onam*. This is a kind of regatta in which boat races take place between thirty or forty rowers in specially decorated "snake" boats.

October

October sees one of India's greatest traditional holidays, differently named according to where it takes place: in the north of India, *Ram Lila*; in the south, *Dussehra*; in Calcutta, *Durga Puja*. This is a series of festivals, which is in effect one long ten-day celebration. It commemorates the slaying of the buffalo-headed demon Mahishasur by Durga (or Parvati, wife of the god Shiva). During the first nine days prayers are recited, and the relevant episodes of the *Ramayana* are recounted and enacted. The tenth day is the major holiday.

One of the main centers is Calcutta, which practically closes down for the ten days to celebrate the festival of *Durga Puja*. The goddess Kali (another form of Durga) is the main deity of the area. According to legend, the body of Durga was cut into pieces; one of her fingers fell here, and a temple was built on the spot in her honor. The present building, on the same site, dates from 1809. It is called Kalighat (from which Calcutta derives its name). The compound is usually spattered with blood from goats that have had their throats slit in order to appease Kali. Whole coconuts are also offered and smashed. On the tenth day, effigies of Ravana, the demon king of Lanka, are burned to celebrate the victory of good over evil, and the return home of the exiled heroes, Rama, his wife Sita, and his brother Lakshamana.

October-November

Diwali is the most important Hindu festival, also known as the "Festival of Lights." It is joyously celebrated for four days (or five, depending on the lunar calendar) in honor of Lakshmi, goddess of prosperity. Each day brings a different ritual, including lamp lighting, bathing, feasting, decorating the house, firecrackers, and gift giving.

The fourth day is the day for finalizing business accounts for the year, and offering worship to Lakshmi. Traditionally, business partners also give each other and their employees presents at *Diwali*, and foreign business partners often neglect this through ignorance. People often gamble at this time to test their luck in the new financial year.

November

At the time of the full moon, traders with horses, bullocks, and caravans of camels gather for an annual fair that includes camel racing and jumping, near the sacred lake of Pushkar, in Rajasthan.

Caught up in the Festival of Color

Traveling anywhere on *Holi,* the Hindu festival of color, usually celebrated in March, is definitely to be avoided as most Indians, regardless of religion, go crazy and hurl colored water, colored powder, and paint over everyone and everything. This is usually followed by offering friends sweets and a pleasant-tasting concoction of milk and ground almonds, liberally laced with *bhang* (hashish), or beer.

Local and Occasional Festivals

Local holidays may include events like *Poshi Punam*, when all little girls are given their first lesson in cooking rice, usually in the form of *kheer* (rice pudding). By the time a girl is considered a woman, she is expected to know at least fifteen different ways of preparing rice.

The Indians love religious *melas* (fairs). Televised worldwide, the *Kumbh Mela* is the largest gathering of people on earth. A great pilgrimage, celebrated with unique fervor, it takes place about every twelve years at the confluence of the holy rivers Ganges and Jumna at Allahabad, in Uttar Pradesh. It is believed that the water here at this time has special properties and healing powers, and that bathing at the festival cures the bather of all sins and sickness, and grants salvation. The elderly go to the *Kumbh Mela* in the hope of dying there, as it is believed that this will give them *moksh*— liberation from the cycle of birth and death. This is also considered true of the holy city of Varanasi (Benares), where it is not uncommon to have to step over dead bodies in the streets. In January and February 2001 over 30 million people from different parts of the world participated in the *Kumbh Mela*.

Religious Devotion Is Everywhere
"*The Sabarimala Hindu pilgrimage was going on in Kerala in December when we were there. We saw men trekking 150 miles to a special forest shrine, in just their dhotis, with gifts for the Gods on their heads.*"
Anya Noakes

Muslim Festivals

The Muslim calendar is lunar, and the major festivals—linked to commands of the Koran or the life of Muhammad—advance around the seasons of the solar year.

The holy month of *Ramadan*, the ninth month of the Islamic year, is observed with prayers and fasting during the hours of daylight. This period of devotion commemorates the revelation of the Koran to the Prophet Muhammad. The end of Ramadan is celebrated by *Id-al-Fitr*, feast of the breaking of the fast.

Muslims also commemorate Abraham's willingness to sacrifice his son Ishmael (according to the Koran) in the feast of *Bakar Id*, also known as *Id al-Adha*, *Id-al-Kurban*, and *al-Id al Kabir*. An animal, usually a goat or a sheep, is sacrificed. Generally the meat is eaten by the celebrants, and some is given to the poor.

Muharram is a ten-day observance that commemorates the martyrdom of Muhammad's grandson, Imam Hussain.

On *Shab-i-Barat*, the Night of Allotment, human deeds are measured and their rewards allotted. Observed only in India, it is celebrated with fireworks. All-night reading of the Koran is followed by a fast the next day.

chapter four

TIME IN

At dawn every morning, all over India, blaring Indian music wakes everyone up. It comes from radios behind Ganesh, or whichever god is being celebrated, in the small Hindu street temples. What with that, and the Muslim call to prayer that crackles from the top of mosques in every town at 5 a.m., there is no chance of sleeping in when traveling in India!

HOME AND FAMILY

Imagine living with ten to fifteen people under the same roof! This is how many Indians live. It is common to have three or even four generations of a family living in one house. There is a total lack of privacy in Indian life, and concepts such as "needing my space" are totally alien to most Indians. Indeed, there is no word for privacy in Indian languages.

Indians wonder at the inhumanity of the Western nuclear family, and cannot understand why Americans and Europeans attempt to move their elders into homes or special communities. This goes against both their sense of community and their respect for elders.

An Indian child is at the same time looked after closely and given relatively little personal attention. Normally an Indian child will sleep in the same room as his or her parents until the age of about twelve. Indians find it difficult to understand why Westerners put a vulnerable young child in a room on their own, almost from birth.

Indian life is characterized by great interdependence, and also deep respect for authority. The father is seen as the head of the household: sons and daughters may live in the house until marriage and beyond, and even at the age of twenty-six a girl might still ask her father, "May I go out to dinner tonight?"

Another feature of Indian middle-class houses is servants who live in. Most foreigners have a mixed reaction to them. They enjoy the luxury of not having to do various jobs in the house, but worry about the "moral" aspect. It should be remembered that this practice provides employment to those who might otherwise be jobless. Relatives from the country may also stay with the family and "earn their keep" by doing housework. Even if the mother cooks, the sons will never be asked to cook, wash the dishes, or clean.

Therefore, when Indian men go abroad to study or work, they have to learn how to shop, cook, clean, and wash their own dishes and clothes. This is why the living standards of Indians away from home may sometimes appear to be lower than their qualifications and family background would suggest, and it may be necessary to tactfully help new arrivals learn these skills for themselves.

Indian cities and villages have an open-air culture. Most services are carried out in the street, including medical and dental treatment, haircutting, laundry, and cooking. When someone is ill they will normally go to hospital, not to a family doctor. Families "register" with a hospital doctor, who accepts them into his care. Most families will never use a pharmacist. For the more affluent there are very good private hospitals and clinics. Beauty parlors and hairdressing salons exist in the cities.

Religion is a vital issue in Indian daily life. Indian homes will have shrines, and believers will mix mostly with people from their own religion. When they meet you, they will expect to talk about their religion and will want to ask about yours. It is very important for the foreigner to have a religion and to be prepared to talk about it. Religion is not private in India in the way that it is in the United States and Britain. For Indians, your belief means you can be trusted, and that you must be treated in an honest way.

The Indians believe in background. It is important for them to know which street their colleagues live on, which school they went to, and what their parents do. They want to know about you, too, and will ask questions that you might consider intrusive. The reason behind it, however, is that they want to know how to "place" you, and then they will know how to treat you, and will respect you. Indians will often volunteer information that you might think is irrelevant, but for them it is extremely important in establishing mutual respect.

HOUSING

Housing is quite varied, and may be luxurious or dilapidated. Infrastructure in some parts of India can be uncertain. Electricity supply is erratic, for example, and power cuts and water shortages are common. More than half of urban Indians live without any form of sewage system. Nearly one-third of city dwellers have no toilet, and 16 percent have no water supply. Most properties however, have water tanks with pumps, electricity generators, and rooms cooled by ceiling fans. If you are looking for long-term accommodation for yourself and your family, you will quickly find the main expatriate areas, where the better housing is located. Because it is not advisable to drive, it is better not to be too far from a supermarket or, if you have children, from schools.

British influence is evident in the bungalows on the greener outskirts of the cities. The middle classes also live in apartments that could be found anywhere in the world. Only the kitchens and bathrooms have their own characteristics.

Indian kitchens are generally quite primitive, and very rarely have running hot water. Where there is no piped gas supply, bottled gas is ordered in advance from suppliers. The rich middle classes usually have a cook and one or two other servants, although some orthodox Hindu families who adhere to strict dietary practices will not entrust the preparation of food to someone who is not of their own caste or  religion. A Brahmin cook is the exception, as the food prepared will be acceptable at religious feasts by other Brahmins. Even in homes where the housewife does her own cooking, she will have a part-time servant who will come in to wash the dishes.

Take Your Shoes Off!
It is customary to take your shoes off when entering a traditional Hindu home. Do as your host does, or ask his advice.

The Indians like to wash in running water, and most take bucket baths. Bathing in a tub of water sullied by one's own dirt is considered disgusting. Bathrooms have a square bathing area sunk about two inches below the rest of the room, as well as a faucet and possibly a shower. The Indians fill up a bucket, crouch, and use a mug to pour water over themselves. The westernized rich, however, may well have at least one bathtub in the house.

Be Prepared for an Indian-Style Toilet

Middle-class homes have Western-style lavatories, but most others will have an Indian-style toilet where you place your feet on either side of a hole and squat. In older parts of cities, several buildings may share this facility. Usually a hole in the ground, it might be two bricks on either side of a pit. There is no toilet paper, as its use is repellent to most Indians. It is generally believed that it is cleaner to use water.

There is usually a tap by the side of the toilet, and a small pot. The business of cleansing takes the form of cold water being splashed by the left hand in the appropriate direction. It is understood that nothing is accepted in the left hand, as it is considered unclean, and never used for eating with. (In rural India, you will see the villagers heading for the fields at dawn with a water pot. Hands are then cleaned with a little mud and water.) If your hosts are well traveled, they may have bought toilet paper specially for you. Better hotels and restaurants will have westernized toilet facilities, but a toilet roll and soap are essential items in your baggage, together with a universal sink plug, as hand basins never seem to have them.

CELEBRATING THE LIFE CYCLE

The most important value for the Indians is respect, whether of self or of others. This involves respecting their culture. The Indians love ritual and protocol, and religious festivals are a vital part of this. Your understanding and appreciation of these rituals will increase their respect for you and demonstrate yours for them.

A good example is Diwali, the festival of light, and the Indian equivalent of Christmas. This is the time for closing accounts, and for giving gifts among employees and business partners. Your failure to understand and recognize this could earn you a reputation for meanness—give a present for Diwali!

Births and weddings require long and elaborate celebrations. An Indian may wish to take four or five weeks off to attend to wedding arrangements. As many as a thousand people may be invited, and the hosts may well spend far more money than they have, going deeply into debt, because they believe it is necessary.

Join In!
An American fundamentalist was asked to attend a Hindu ceremony. He was invited to wear a garland, to take part in a coconut ceremony, and to drink coconut milk. Because his beliefs weren't in accord with Hindu rituals, he politely excused himself from joining in the ceremonies. But in doing so he forfeited the trust and confidence of his Indian colleagues.

Among Hindus, rituals begin before birth. As the child grows older, rites are undertaken for important stages of development. There is a ritual for the first time the child eats solid food, which is usually rice. The first haircutting, where the hair is completely shaved off, is celebrated for a young boy, and for a girl a purification rite is carried out after the first menstruation. Prayers are offered to Sarasvati, the goddess of learning, before a child starts school; there is the sacred thread ceremony for adolescent boys of the first three castes; and then comes marriage. This is followed by blessings upon a pregnancy, in the hope of producing a male child, as well as to ensure a successful delivery and the child's survival during the dangerous first six days after birth.

Among the Hindus, generally speaking, the wife performs the daily *puja* (prayers). Statues of the gods (silver if you are well off and brass if you are not) are bathed and dressed. Offerings of fruit and flowers are made to them in a small shrine in the house. The wife also makes offerings to local snakes, trees, or spirits (benevolent and malevolent) dwelling in her own garden, at crossroads, or in other magical places in the community. The men perform a similar *puja* before starting work.

A Good Death
Last of all are the funeral rites, cremation, and, if possible, the sprinkling of ashes in a holy river such as the Ganges (Ganga). Ganges water is carried by Hindus around the world, as it should be the last thing that is put into the mouth when a Hindu dies.

Hindus are generally cremated on open wooden pyres, the size of which depends on the social status of the family. The most famous "burning ghats" are at Varanasi (Benares). The recent funeral pyre constructed to cremate an ex-president of India, a Sikh, used four quintals (882 lbs, or 400 kilos) of wood, some of it precious sandalwood. Seven tins (40 lbs, or 18 kilos, each) of pure *ghee* (clarified butter), mixed with 66 lbs (30 kilos) of *havan samagri* (herbs and spices used in Vedic ceremonies), were thrown on to the flames while Brahmin priests chanted verses from the *Vedas.* This was accompanied by a twenty-one-gun salute and the sounding of the Last Post—a curious cocktail of East and West.

Annual offerings to dead ancestors include a mixture of rice and sesame seeds. These are traditionally offered by the eldest male child to ensure that the ghost of his father will pass from limbo into rebirth.

Muslims are generally buried; the Taj Mahal in Agra, built from white marble and inlaid with gemstones, is a beautiful example of a mausoleum in the Indo-Islamic style. It was built in the seventeenth century by the Mogul emperor Shah Jahan for his cherished wife, Mumtaz Mahal.

The Parsis expose their dead on platforms inside high, open "Towers of Silence," to be devoured by vultures.

SOCIAL RELATIONS AND OCCUPATIONS

Various communities have traditionally pursued carefully defined occupations. The Punjabis are considered to be excellent farmers. The Marwaris, a small, closely knit community originally from the western state of Rajasthan, are industrialists and moneylenders. The Chettiyars are like the Marwaris but are in the south, mainly in Chennai (Madras). The Tamils from South India traditionally become bureaucrats. Gujaratis are traders and merchants. The westernized Parsis can be found among the business people you are likely to meet in Mumbai (Bombay) or Gujarat. The Jains, who traditionally served as accountants to the Muslim rulers, continue in money management, and also account for half the world's trade in small, polished diamonds.

All in a Name

In India, no more than a name is needed to "place" anybody. A name identifies an individual as coming from a specific community whose attributes are assumed in advance. For example, you are told that the family name of a Brahmin is Divedi. This "places" this individual as coming from a community where two *Vedas* were studied. If three *Vedas* were studied the name would be Trivedi, or if four, Chaturvedi.

Some south Indian groups have a very intricate naming system. Take, for example, someone called R. V. Ramamurthy. Ramamurthy will be the personal name, and the initials will denote the name of the ancestral village and the father. Certain Parsis derive their names from their occupation, for example, Mr. Doctor or Mr. Mistry (mechanic).

FAMILY RELATIONSHIPS

In traditional homes, there is a formal, institutionalized code of conduct for family members. Everyone knows their place and how to behave. People rarely say "please" or "thank you," as there is no need. This is also carried into the workplace (apart from the airlines, which is the only context in which you are likely to hear these words). Everything is prescribed, from the way the young members of the family greet the elders—such as whose feet must be touched in the morning and in which order—to how many saris and cooking utensils should be included in a dowry. The eldest married lady of the house reigns supreme, and rules over her sisters and daughters-in-law with a rod of iron.

Relationships are self-evident from the names used; for example, *Dada*, paternal grandfather, and *Dadi*, paternal grandmother; *Nana*, maternal grandfather, and *Nani*, maternal grandmother; *Taya*, father's elder brother, and *Tayi*, his wife; *Chacha*, father's younger brother, and *Chachi*, his wife; *Devar*, husband's younger brother, and *Devarani*, his wife.

The Indian form of Mr. and Mrs. is *Shri* and *Shrimati* (abbreviated to *Smt*). Sikh men have the name Singh (lion) and Sikh women have Kaur (princess) after their personal name, followed by the family name, for example, Sher Singh Aluwalia or Gurmeet Kaur Saund. Muslim men will often refer to their wife as *Begum*, a Muslim woman of high rank. The westernized Parsis use Mr. and Mrs.

A Wife Never Says Her Husband's Name

In no circumstances will an Indian wife say her husband's name aloud, as it is considered disrespectful. When addressing him, she will use all manner of oblique references such as *"ji"* or "look here" or "hello" and in some extreme cases will refer to him as the father of her child!

MARRIAGE

In the days before people moved into towns, a marriage would be arranged from among the people you knew, or through the local barber or priest. Now, among the middle classes, marriages are often arranged through classified advertisements in the personal columns of Sunday newspapers, and love matches are increasing. There are still very few interreligious or intercaste marriages, however, and the advertisements reflect this.

Hindus, Sikhs, Muslims, and Christians are married by priests. Hindu marriages are usually performed at home by walking seven times around a ceremonial holy fire.

Wealth is flaunted at Indian weddings, which are spectacular, theatrical events, the celebrations generally lasting least three days. A Hindu bridegroom, accompanied by his entourage and a brass band, rides a white charger to his bride's home.

The Bindi

Applying the traditional *bindi*, or dot, to the forehead of both bride and groom, using a special red powder, is part of a Hindu marriage ceremony. The husband also applies powder along the parting of the hair of his bride to signify that she is married. Today the dot has become a fashion item among young women, now that peel-and-stick *bindis* of every shade and hue are generally available!

Legislation in recent years now gives a woman equal status with a man. Under the 1956 Hindu Succession Act, all Hindu and Sikh women have the right to inherit ancestral property. In reality, though, women are still treated as second-class citizens and some organizations pay only lip service to equal opportunities. But many women do go to work. This is becoming more common in the cities, for economic reasons. Women are becoming far more vocal and make demands they never would have before. Their expectations have been raised through education and exposure to Western ideas through the media. Many women now hold important positions in international companies operating in India.

PHYSICAL CONTACT

Indians are not "touchy-feely," and disapprove of public displays of affection between the sexes. Physical contact between men and women, even the simplest hug or kiss, is considered provocative behavior, and is likely to invite rough treatment in most of India. Things are more relaxed in Goa, although even there discretion is advised, as it is also a popular holiday destination for visitors from other Indian states.

Shaking hands with the opposite sex is another potential minefield. It is not socially acceptable for an Indian woman to be touched by any male other than her husband or son, and then by her husband only in private. So males should not shake hands with an Indian woman unless she offers it first. This goes for Western-style dancing as well. If you are invited to a disco or restaurant where there is dancing, it's a good idea to check with your host as to the custom. Among the young these conventions are starting to change.

You often see men holding hands and occasionally, much to the indignation of a Western male, an Indian man will persist in holding his hand as a bonding gesture. This has no sexual overtones whatsoever.

IZZAT, OR SAVING FACE

There are some aspects of marriage that can be troublesome, particularly for women. These are the consequences of *izzat,* which has to do with self-respect and saving face

One aspect is the dowry. Dowries are now illegal, and yet parents, irrespective of religion, feel that they have to provide for their daughters, and to be seen to do so by the rest of the community. They feel obliged to spend huge amounts of money, and in some cases will put themselves deeply into debt. This is a subject not to be discussed.

After this might come a tragic "dowry death." As India's own statistics show, one of these occurs every hundred minutes, when in-laws cause the death of a new bride if they decide she has not brought a sufficiently large dowry. This is often described as a "kitchen" death, with the unlikely story that kerosene, the most common fuel used for cooking, somehow splashed on to the daughter-in-law and burned her to death before anyone could save her. A consequence of this is that every couple wants to have a male child.

Izzat also means that it is difficult for a woman to instigate divorce proceedings, whatever her religion. Indeed, the late Prime Minister, Rajiv Gandhi, bowed to Muslim fundamentalist demands that Muslim women should not be subject to civil laws concerning divorce. Saving face is so important that a man will go to great lengths, even bribing the court officials, to delay the proceedings if his wife has asked for a divorce. In this way, he ensures that if a divorce is imminent it is he who asks for it.

The attitude toward a widow is that she must be a harbinger of bad luck, or otherwise her husband would not have died. Old women in the community describe the widow as "the one who ate her husband." As soon as her husband dies her glass bangles are smashed, and her *bindi* is wiped off. In certain groups, the custom of shaving her head still continues.

In orthodox families, widows are not allowed anywhere near newlyweds, or welcomed at auspicious gatherings. It is no wonder that *sati*— self-immolation on her husband's funeral pyre— is considered an option in villages, as once she has made up her mind to carry this out the widow is treated as a goddess, and hundreds of people visit the site of the pyre. Outlawed in the nineteenth century, the practice still continues. It should be stressed, however, that Indian society in general, and the government of India in particular, are strictly against the practice of *sati*, which has been declared a criminal offense.

SUPERSTITION

The Indians in general are very superstitious. Every village has a venerated *pundit,* a priest, and an astrologer. They are not only important for weddings, but are also consulted before the start of any business venture. Indians are obsessed with the notion that someone might cast a *nazar,* or "evil eye," on them, and take precautions to safeguard themselves against this. For instance, it is customary for a baby to have a black spot placed behind the ears, so that people will notice this rather than the beauty of the child. Buildings under construction have a horrific face painted on a large pot, or a demonic figure displayed on the front, to scare away evil spirits. If someone does fall victim to *nazar,* then homegrown remedies are used. As a last resort, prayers and various activities are conducted by the local priest.

ASTROLOGY

Traditional beliefs can sometimes interfere with Western values at the level of business. Imagine that you want an appointment to sign an agreement with an Indian colleague who insists on April 23, a date that is not convenient for you. He is insistent, but will never tell you the reason: he has consulted an astrologer, who has divined that April 23 is the most auspicious day for signature. What may appear to you to be stubborn and uncooperative behavior is something else entirely.

Astrology may also determine auspicious or inauspicious days for meetings or travel. Whatever your own views on the matter, you should be aware that a different set of variables comes into play.

DRESS

The Indians are quite conservative in their dress, and expect you to dress neatly and modestly. What passes for casual in the West is often too casual in India, and may be considered unkempt. Many Indians are shocked and embarrassed to be faced with a backpacker in jeans and a tee shirt. It is a good idea to err on the side of formality during the day, and you should certainly have smart formal wear for public evening occasions, as affluent, middle-class Indians are very fashion conscious.

Dressing correctly will avoid harassment. Women should not wear revealing clothes, especially in Muslim areas, which call for more restraint in modes of dress. The amount of harassment received by a Western woman is directly related to the amount of flesh she is exposing. Knee-length skirts or long trousers are suitable. Plunging necklines, strapless tops, and going without a bra will invite remarks and stares, so however hot it gets you should keep your shoulders and upper arms covered, as these are considered particularly erotic by Indian men.

Women might consider adopting a popular local dress, *salwar* and *kameez*—baggy trousers and long-sleeved tunic. These are comfortable and inexpensive, and are available ready-made in beautiful materials and designs. A *duppatta* (scarf) draped over your shoulder, chest, and, when necessary, head, suggests modesty and virtue. However, although a woman who adopts Indian styles may attract less hassle from men, the

Indians often don't feel particularly comfortable with Europeans dressing in this way, and many find the sight of a Western woman wearing a sari either shocking or ridiculous.

People are more relaxed about men's dress, although they can be similarly disturbed to see a Western man in a *dhoti,* or loincloth, or skimpy shorts, or even Indian caps and turbans.

Whether you are male or female, dressing in modest, conventional Western dress will command respect in India. If visiting houses or temples, you should remove your shoes unless told not to. It is also polite to cover your head in sacred places.

HOSPITALITY

The Indians as a group are warm, hospitable people, who take every opportunity to be friendly to foreigners, sometimes uncomfortably so. They will press food and drink on you, and it may be that you do not want it. Refuse at first then, if you can, accept it the second or third time it is offered. The best policy if you really do not want what is being offered is to smile, politely and firmly say "no," and explain that you have just eaten.

Quite often, even total strangers will ask you to visit them at home, and will persist until you agree. It's best to respond with: "Oh yes, we would love to come one day." You are then expected to forget all about it! They will be surprised if you take their offer at face value and turn up. If you really wish to accept, it is wise to clarify this and to arrange a firm date and time. They may want to go to some lengths to prepare a meal for you, so don't drop in without notice.

GREETINGS

Indians generally greet each other and say goodbye with palms held together as if saying prayers, and say *"namaste,"* which literally means, "I recognize the self in you." For Hindi speakers this is usually followed by *"kya hal hai?"* ("how is your health?"); *"teak taak"* (all right) and in both cases the "t" is aspirated. *"Teak hai"* or *"achha"* (okay) is used for everything from answering a general enquiry to an affirmation that the road is clear ahead.

Muslims use the stylized greeting, *"salaam aleikum"* ("peace be upon you"), the reply being *"aleikum assalaam"* ("and on you, peace"). If in doubt it is quite safe just to say "hello" with a smile. The Sikh greeting is *"sat sri akal."* It is polite to greet the eldest person first.

GIFT GIVING

There is no tradition of taking a gift if you are invited to visit an Indian family, but flowers or a present of anything American or European is always appreciated, particularly chocolate, or cosmetics for the women of the household. The very best gift you can take a business partner is a bottle of Scotch whisky (cheaper at duty-free on arrival), although it may not be welcome if they are Muslim. Red and green or yellow gifts will be positively received, as these are lucky colors in India. Gifts are not normally opened in the presence of the giver.

Gifts to be avoided include frangipani (used at funerals) and anything black or white (note this when choosing wrapping paper), which are regarded as unlucky colors. If you are giving money, it should always be an uneven number, for example 101, not 100 rupees. Don't give cowhide products to Hindus. Muslims consider pigs, dogs, and amphibians unclean, so don't give them toys resembling these, or pigskin or lizardskin products, or pictures of these animals.

TABOO SUBJECTS

It's best to avoid politics and specifically Indian concerns such as poverty, dowries, dowry deaths, *sati*, and similar subjects that might cause embarrassment. There is still plenty to discuss if you stick to generally uncontroversial topics such as history, culture, art, food, family, and so on.

Subjects that may be taboo in the West, such as illness and death, are discussed more openly in India. Sex, however, together with homosexuality and lesbianism, is not openly discussed.

Traditionally, at parties, middle-class women would sit together drinking Coca Cola and discussing the latest film or the servant problem, while the men drank whisky and cracked schoolboy jokes with sexual overtones. This, too, is changing in non-orthodox circles.

INDIAN HUMOR

It is not easy for the Indians to laugh at themselves, as they take themselves very seriously. On the whole, people enjoy slapstick humor and will laugh merrily at someone else's misfortune, such as slipping on a banana skin. Traditionalists hate the idea of caricatures of people they respect, although it is increasingly fashionable to make fun of politicians. Only a few people appreciate sardonic or "dark" humor. Foreigners may find much Indian humor rather simple and lacking in subtlety.

FOOD & DRINK

FOOD

Indian cuisine is very diverse, so if you are adventurous you will be delighted with the many tastes and flavors to be tried. The Indians love eating out, and in the main city centers there is a wide range of eating places with every kind of food available, from expensive Western-style and Chinese restaurants to little stalls selling *chaat,* a fiery mixture of fruit and vegetables. But do remember, if you don't want fiery food, it is important to ask for something that has no chilies in it. Your phrase book will tell you that *garam* is the word for hot, but that means its temperature! Many foreigners who are wary of fiery food ask for something that is not *"garam,"* and end up with cold food full of chilies! Western-style food is available in luxury hotels, British-style clubs, and finer restaurants. If you are invited out to eat, the meal is likely to be in one of these, and the fare similar to that in the West.

You can eat well, cheaply, and safely all over India. But it isn't always easy to tell whether food has been hygienically prepared, and you can be unlucky, so be careful to choose something that is freshly and thoroughly cooked, and very hot. The roadside restaurant *(dhaba)* is often just a basic shelter created out of odd boards and sheets of galvanized iron, with wooden tables and benches. Food is cooked on a brazier and is delicious. In Goa, the restaurants and shacks, the temporary huts that serve excellent food and drink on the beaches during the tourist season, are generally open until midnight, and a few are open all night.

Indian sweet stalls are a colorful extravaganza of sticky confections, with different regional varieties. Most Indian women love these sweets and many suffer from sugar diabetes. Note that, in Indian culture, to be overweight is considered healthy. In a country where many people go hungry, it is a sure sign of wealth.

Meals of the Day

Morning tea is taken between 6:00 a.m. and 7:00 a.m. Depending on which part of India you are in, breakfast can be *mathis* (fried savory biscuits) and *jalebis* (sticky, syrupy, fried sweets) in the

north, *idli* and *sambhar* (steamed rice cakes and
lentils) or *dosas*, huge, crispy rice pancakes,
served with delicious hot coffee in the south. *Pau
roti* (white bread) is generally available.
Restaurants will serve eggs in a number of ways,
including single fried (sunny-side up) or double
fried. Rumble tumble (scrambled) should be
avoided as the eggs might be of questionable age
and origin!

Lunch is between 1:00 p.m. and 2:00 p.m., and
consists of rice and curry. Dinner is usually
served at about 8:30 p.m. However, dining late,
like serving Scotch whisky and French wines, is a
status symbol in India.

If you are invited to an Indian home, it is
acceptable, or even expected, that you will arrive
fifteen to thirty minutes late. If you know you
can't tolerate spicy food, it is best to say
beforehand, "I'd love to come and see you, but
my stomach gets a bit upset with spicy food." It is
far better to do this than to sit there and refuse
the food, as the hostess will usually have gone to
a lot of trouble to prepare it.

Family and friends eat sitting around the
dining table, or the food may be served buffet-
style for a larger gathering. A complete meal will
consist of six traditional items: *dal* (split lentils),
rice, vegetables, yogurt, and chutney, *roti* or
chappati (flat, unleavened bread, generally baked,

not fried); other varieties include *puri, paratha,* and *naan.* The last two may be baked in a *tandoor* (a deep oven with live coals). *Chappatis* made of freshly kneaded dough are rolled out thinly and cooked on a hot *tawa* (griddle), then toasted until puffed up on an open fire. Hindus cook their *chappatis* on a convex *tawa,* and Muslims on a concave one. "Modern" Indians sometimes serve soup as a first course at dinner. Meat is becoming increasingly popular in homes and the more expensive restaurants, but a large proportion of Hindus are vegetarian. A lavish vegetarian meal consists of thirty-three different preparations of vegetables and thirty-three different Indian sweets.

The Left Hand is Unclean

The left hand is considered unclean, so taking or eating anything with the left hand should be avoided.

You generally help yourself, or you may be served with a small amount of each of the numerous dishes and some form of bread. A small piece should be torn off and used (with the right hand) to scoop up the vegetable or curry. The south Indians have made the eating of rice and *sambhar,* a regional dish of lentils, into a fine art. The rice and lentils are mixed into little balls and then dexterously popped into the mouth.

Dessert is often fruit in custard, or *kheer* (rice pudding), or sticky sweets flavored with cardamom, nutmeg, saffron, and other spices, and covered with silver leaf. In summer you will be served with *kulfi* and *faluda,* Indian ice cream and sweet noodles flavored with saffron and rose water, which are quite delicious.

The meal usually ends with *paan,* a national obsession. This consists of a handful of areca (betel) nut, lime, spices, and condiments, all wrapped in fresh betel leaf, placed in the mouth and chewed. It is considered to be a digestive.

Paan Stalls

Stalls selling *paan* are to be found everywhere, crammed into any available space, and outside restaurants. You can get designer *paan,* such as *sadda* (plain), *mitha* (sweet), or filled with your favorite chewing tobacco or cocaine, and covered with gold or silver leaf. It is customary to serve a bridegroom with a special *paan* on his wedding night. Aptly named *palang tor* (bed-breaker), it supposedly contains aphrodisiacs. Be careful if you decide to try a *paan,* as the woody betel nut can be a tooth-breaker for unaccustomed Westerners. When you have finished chewing, the correct protocol is to spit out the juice to add to the other orange stains spattering the streets.

Paan stalls often have a rope with a lighted end hanging on a hook so that customers can light their cigarette or *bidi* (pronounced beerie). *Bidis* are small, vile-smelling, indigenous cigarettes that are wrapped in a cheap grade of tobacco leaf.

ETIQUETTE—DOS AND DON'TS

- Do not refuse refreshment in India without good reason, as this is seen as an insult. It is customary to refuse the first offer, but to accept the second or third. A good way to thank your hosts is to invite them out to a meal in a restaurant in return.

- Always wash your hands both before and after a meal. Rinsing your mouth out is also a Hindu custom.

- In traditional families, the guests and the men are served first, and the women eat afterward.

- As a foreigner you might be offered a fork, but most people eat with their fingers, using the right hand only. Never eat with your left hand, although it is acceptable to pass plates with it.

- If asked to pass the salt, don't place it in the hand of the person asking for it, as this is considered bad luck.

- Be aware that food has a ritual quality in India. It is seen as pure, and becomes polluted when you touch it. If you touch a communal dish with your hands, other diners may avoid it. Never offer food from your plate, for this same reason. If drinking water from a communal vessel, lips must not touch it.

- Remember that much of India is vegetarian, that Hindus and Sikhs don't eat beef, and that Muslims don't eat pork.

DRINK

It is not safe to drink unsterilized water in India (see Prevention is Better than Cure, in Chapter 7). Indians themselves usually drink water with their meals, but if you refuse it your hosts will not be offended. You may be offered *nimboo pani*—fresh, old-fashioned lemonade or lime juice—or *lassi,* a yogurt drink. In both cases, check that it has been made with cooled boiled water. Do not ask for ice. Of course, there is always tea or coffee, and there are wonderful fruit juices and flavored milk drinks.

Tea Drinking

India is the world's largest tea producer and in common with Britain, *chai* (tea) is its number one beverage. *Chai* will be offered to you at all times, everywhere you go in India. *Dhabas* (roadside restaurants) provide delicious cups of *masala* tea, which is generally milky, sweet, and flavored with cardamom and other spices such as ginger, cinnamon, and cloves.

How the British Got Hooked

British associations with Indian tea go back to 1662, when Queen Catherine, the wife of Charles II, introduced tea drinking to the English as a social habit, having brought chests of tea with her as part of her dowry.

Alcohol

Indian beer is excellent, and so is the rum; gin is passable. Indian whisky is reasonable at the top of the range, less so at the bottom. Goa's *Urak,* similar to the so-called snake juice, is legally and illegally distilled all over India, and is said to be stomach-searing.

Indians enjoy drinking, and more women are now doing so, but alcohol is not usually served at meal times in an Indian home. People generally drink in restaurants and clubs, and pub or bar culture is growing in major cities like Mumbai (Bombay) and Bangalore. In Goa, which is different from any other state in India, there are several bars on every street. Excise duty is low, and excellent, chilled, lagerlike beer is available very cheaply in most bars, and for three times the price in the five-star hotels. The local *fenny* (somewhat like cheap *eau de vie*) is distilled both from coconut and the cashew apple, and is much loved by the locals; if you want to take it out of the state you must get a permit.

There is prohibition in Gujarat, which has, inevitably, spawned an illegal market in liquor. Indeed, around Ahmadabad a once nomadic tribe, the Charas, distill a cheap liquor, also known as Charas. Foreigners can get a permit to drink in a dry state.

chapter six

TIME OUT

ENCOUNTERING POVERTY

Most foreigners are horrified and upset by the poverty that is apparent everywhere in India, and by the huge differences between rich and poor. Miles of shantytowns, populated by families living in lean-tos and shacks, have grown up on the outskirts of major cities, near airports, and in the scrub beside the railway. People can even be found sleeping on the raised divide in the middle of busy roads in city centers. Not very far away can be found the big houses, well-tended gardens, and luxury cars of the well-to-do.

The inequality of wealth in India poses more problems for Westerners than for most Indians. It's worth remembering that it is the Indians' belief in reincarnation and *karma*, rather than coldness in the face of human suffering, which is how it may appear, that protects them from distress in the face of poverty. Charity is, however, part of life in India.

Westerners find India a cheap country to live in, but it's important to remember that wages are not high, and even a middle-class Indian, who would expect to run a household on 3,000 rupees ($64 or £42) a month, may find life expensive.

At street level, India is a cash economy, and street vendors, rickshaw owners, taxi drivers, etc., often claim they have no change. Money is obviously very important in this country of extreme poverty and enormous wealth. You cannot blame people for trying to earn a few extra rupees, so it's better to have the right money. Carry plenty of small change.

Dealing with Beggars

Begging is a fact of life in India, and something a visitor has to contend with. The truth is that India has had several good harvests and few people starve, certainly not in the villages where the majority of the population lives. In cities and the major tourist centers, begging is often a racket and organized in gangs, with the organizer taking the major share.

Beggars can be very pushy, and it is hard to resist the appeals of a small child, or to be unmoved by the suffering around you. But if you give money, a crowd will quickly gather and you will be bombarded by requests. This can be quite frightening. It is better, although sad, to ignore beggars and comply with the Indian concept of *karma*. You can, of course, give to recognized charities. If you feel you must help more directly, give some food, such as small snacks, fruit, or sweets. Anything you do give should be given as you leave, or you will not be left alone.

There are always new ways to relieve you of your money. Watch out for a scam that can happen outside temples: if you have a free hand, someone may slam a bangle on it and then shout for payment. Be firm in your refusal, or keep your hands in your pockets!

You may be inundated with offers to change money on the black market. But, since the convertibility of the Indian rupee in 1992, there is very little premium in this and it is therefore not worth the risk. It is, of course, illegal.

CROWDS, AND LACK OF PRIVACY

Lack of privacy will permeate your life in India. It is a collectivist culture, and individual space is not a recognized concept, let alone seen as positive or important. People like to be in groups, and may even feel sorry for you if you are on your own. Expect to draw a  crowd wherever you go. Indians are simply curious about you as a foreigner, and have no inhibitions about staring, asking questions, or just hanging around you. There is little you can do, but understanding it for what it is may help you to smile and tolerate it.

Instant Celebrity
"Traveling in Tamil Nadu, we came out of the temple and went to have something to eat in a nearby restaurant. Within minutes, a crowd six deep had gathered to watch us. As it is just friendly curiosity, all you can do is smile and put up with it."
Member of a group traveling through India

TIPPING

In India you tip not so much for good service received, but to open doors or get things done (see Corruption is Relative, in Chapter 8). Tipping is not necessary in the cheaper restaurants, family-run businesses, and taxis. However, if you are going to visit an establishment frequently, a program of unexpected and intermittent tips will ensure that standards are kept up.

SHOPPING

India assails all your senses. You will encounter a vibrant blaze of colors, blasting heat and dust, and exotic scents of fruits and vegetables—huge mounds of mangoes, watermelons, limes, ginger, and yard-long squash. There are flowers—jasmine, tuberoses, marigolds, and roses; spices—great piles of turmeric, chili, cinnamon, cardamom, and sandalwood; and, of course, incense everywhere. Note that it is considered impolite to sniff and handle flowers at a market.

Markets tend to be in the older parts of the cities. They are organized by commodity, so spices are sold in one street, clothes in another, and so on. There are entire streets selling gold or silver jewelry, gemstones, or pearls.

In the markets, fish and meat are sold in separate areas, and meat is butchered in different ways to suit religious requirements. *Halal* (killed slowly according to Allah's laws) for the Muslim community, and *jhataka* (swift) for the Hindus and Sikhs. Meat is displayed by hanging carcasses in open stalls, and is invariably covered with flies. You can get a fresh chicken by choosing one of the caged birds under the stall and having it killed in front of you.

General stores and pharmacists sell almost everything else you will need, from medicines and cosmetics to toilet rolls and instant coffee. Different stores may specialize in different commodities. Shops are generally open from 9:00 a.m. to 1:00 p.m. and from 4:00 p.m. to 9:00 p.m.

Be alert when shopping, and do not rely on

shopkeepers' descriptions of quality. Prices are usually fixed in large shops, but do try to bargain in the markets.

Jewelry

Of all the decorative arts in India, jewelry is the most universally interesting and beautiful. Filigree work, which disappeared in Europe after the end of the Roman Empire and was introduced again by the Moors in the fifteenth century, was never lost in India. Indian silver jewelry is also distinct for its embedded semiprecious stones, much of it made in Rajasthan. Hyderabad is one of the world's leading centers for pearls.

Beware of Tricksters
Be very careful to check the authenticity of goods. Do some research if you're planning to make a serious investment, or to buy anything in quantity, or clever tricksters will ensure you arrive home to find your fine rubies are pieces of colored glass.

Handicrafts and Textiles

Every state has a government handicrafts emporium, which is a good place to visit. Quality there is usually reliable, and prices are fixed.

Handicrafts on sale include religious sculpture and painting, brass work, bronzes, cane work, pottery, woodwork—sandalwood carvings from Karnataka, rosewood from Kerala and Chennai (Madras), walnut from Kashmir—or leather goods—bags and shoes are a good buy. Other items to consider are musical instruments from Orissa, papier-mâché from Kashmir, silks, hand-made paper, perfumes, soap, tea, and spices.

India offers a wide variety of textiles, and its silks, cottons, and wools rank among the best in the world. Indian cotton is much lighter than European, and is well made and cheap. If you fancy something more glamorous, you can choose from the famed Varanasi silk brocades; Ikat cloth, where the threads are tie-dyed before weaving; soft, silky Pashmina shawls from Kashmir; and the distinctive Rajasthani mirrored and embroidered cotton. Many cities,

Mumbai (Bombay) in particular, have markets selling wonderful materials that you can have made into clothes in no time by local tailors—they can copy the design of any piece of clothing

you bring with you. Carpets, although bulky, are a popular purchase, and Darjeeling is one of the places to buy them.

Spend Your Rupees!

It is illegal to take Indian currency out of the country, which means that you cannot even spend it in the duty-free shops. Any remaining rupees you have at the end of your visit can be changed back at the airport as long as you have the original encashment receipt, valid for three months.

Foreigners are expected to pay all hotel, air, and rail invoices in foreign currency. Rupees are accepted if they are accompanied by the encashment certificate as proof that they have been purchased from an authorized dealer.

SOCIAL AND CULTURAL LIFE

Traditional dance, theater, and music are popular, and there is always some sort of religious festival going on in India (see Holidays and Festivals, in Chapter 2).

India has a free national and regional press and broadcasting system, in spite of some backlash by Hindu fundamentalist groups. For an overview of Indian news in English, *The Times of India* is the best source. A key weekly magazine is the distinguished Bengal-based *The Statesman*.

Classical Indian Dancing

Visitors should make every effort
to watch a performance of
classical Indian dancing, which can
usually be found in any large city.
One of the most highly developed
arts of Indian culture, dancing was an
integral part of the Sanskrit dramas, a
mode of worship performed in the
inner shrines of every temple, and a
courtly pastime. It has remained
remarkably free of outside influence, and is
notable for its expressive hand movements,
graceful turning and swaying, and subtle rhythms.

Welcome to Bollywood

Films play a tremendously important role in
everyday life, so much so that you can't expect to
understand Indian culture fully without having
seen a Hindi film. The Indians are obsessed by
film stars, and hold them in very high esteem.

The Indian film industry, affectionately
known as "Bollywood," of which Mumbai
(Bombay) is the capital, is second only to
America's Hollywood in output, turning out over
a thousand films a year. The majority of films are
produced to a *masala* or "mixed spice" formula
with three vital ingredients: music, violence, and
romance. Although most of these simply offer

cheap escapism for the masses, the industry has produced some superb directors. Foremost among them was Satyajit Ray, who gained international recognition with *Pather Panjali*. A popular film star who enters politics can be assured of instant success.

The Indian film censors have recently allowed kissing to be shown in Indian films; such scenes were previously allowed only in foreign movies. Nudity is still prohibited, however, so there is a healthy black market in videos. Everything North American is coveted, and *Dynasty* and *Dallas* are used as role models for the Indian elite. Teenagers worship *Baywatch*, and the whole family sits down for *The Bold and the Beautiful*.

Western Women's Ways

"While staying on a houseboat in Kashmir, I was invited to see the film Mona Lisa, *showing in English at the local cinema. It was only when the lights went up at the end that I noticed I was the only woman, and the only Westerner, in the place. As I got up to leave, my friend restrained me. Although, to me, the film was not overly daring by Western standards, to a Muslim audience it was highly titillating, and he was concerned for my safety. As the film had just shown, Western women were up for it."*

Nicki Grihault

Literary Traditions

India has a strong literary tradition in English. While the British have been criticized for belittling Indian culture and portraying their own as being superior, the fact remains that British missionaries set up excellent schools in India and gave the privileged few an education that would not otherwise have been available. They made it possible for generations of Indian writers and poets to tell the world about India. Some internationally known authors are R. K. Narayan, Arundhati Roy, Salman Rushdie, and Vikram Seth.

Sport

The national sport is hockey. All Indians have a passion for cricket, and tennis is also extremely popular. Otherwise, interests often vary by state or region. Polo, for instance, is the traditional sport of Ladakh and Delhi.

An "Open" Society

Unlike many other so-called Third World countries, India is an open society where locals and foreigners can generally move about freely. Foreign correspondents will tell you that they are not followed around by men in cars, as happens elsewhere. The Indian government does not censor transmissions to outside news agencies, and the Internet is gaining momentum.

However, religion and tradition are strong social forces preventing the kind of intermixing of men and women that is usual in Western countries. This results in the majority of adult males, both single and married, in many areas using prostitutes. If you are a man traveling alone, you may well be invited to experience this aspect of city life. The "cages" of Mumbai (Bombay)—a whole street where prostitutes are on show behind bars—are famous. The social taboo on openness about these matters has meant there has been an ineffectual response to the problem of AIDS, which is now becoming quite serious in India.

TRAVEL AND TRANSPORT

India has the third-largest road network in the world at 1.9 million miles (3.1 million km). Only half is surfaced and only 4 percent conforms to international structural norms. It also has the world's second-largest rail network, which is the world's largest civilian employer, with 16 million workers. India's domestic airlines provide a hundred domestic flights daily.

Whether you are visiting India on business or for pleasure, traveling will be involved, and will bring you face to face with bureaucracy, Indian attitudes toward time-keeping, and so on.

Air

The huge size of India, and the frequency of the domestic service, means internal air travel is a common way to get around, particularly as trains tend to be slow. The main domestic airlines are Indian Airlines and Vayudoot. You need to book well in advance to travel on these, especially before major festivals, when families tend to get together to celebrate. Even if you do, there is heavy demand on local flights, which often results in overbooking, delays, and cancellation without notice, so be prepared for this. During the winter months, flights are frequently subject to delay due to fog, particularly those originating from Delhi. To minimize inconvenience, it is essential to reconfirm domestic and international flights and to confirm departure times.

On arrival at the airport, take all luggage to go in the hold to be scanned and security-tagged prior to check-in. You can expect further security checks before boarding, and you will probably be required to identify your baggage lined up with everybody else's on the tarmac before it goes into the hold. Failure to do so will result in its being left behind.

Airport tax is payable prior to international departure. If this has not been paid with your airfare, then remember to check the cost and keep aside the correct amount of rupees.

Railways

A long train journey is a "must" to gain a flavor of
a country of such diverse traditions and customs.
It can be a very pleasant experience to travel by
comfortable, air-conditioned class, or on one of
the special trains, such as the "Palace on Wheels,"
where you'll be treated like a Maharaja.

Train journeys are where the wheels of Indian
bureaucracy come into their own. Bookings
should be made in advance. When you arrive at
the correct carriage you'll find your name on a
typed list, stuck on the window. Increasingly,
however, reservations are being computerized.

Short journeys by train can also be romantic
and fun, such as Delhi to Agra, or Mumbai
(Bombay) to Pune. Local trains carrying
commuters, however, are to be avoided in the rush
hour, when they are extremely crowded.

No train in India travels fast, but at least the
mail and express trains keep traveling most of the
time, and so tend to be faster and more punctual
than the passenger trains
that stop,
sometimes for
long periods, at
every town and
city. The
INDRAIL pass
allows visitors

unlimited travel across the country and greater convenience, and *Trains at a Glance,* which can be bought at Indian station bookstalls, is helpful in planning journeys. Women traveling alone can request seats in an all-women carriage, which can make things easier.

Chain Your Luggage!

The most popular item sold at railway stations is a chain and padlock, to ensure that no one walks off with your suitcase during the night while you are asleep. If it's not chained, don't sleep.

Road

As a general rule, don't drive! In the cities the traffic is chaotic, and the rules of the road, as we know them, seem nonexistent. Also, an accident can involve you in huge problems legally, even if it is not your fault. Leave the driving to local drivers. It is much better to hire a car with a driver, or to take local taxis, than to drive yourself.

You can use the local buses to get around, although sometimes these are almost impossibly crowded. Most cities have cycle rickshaws and the occasional *tonga* (horse-drawn carriage). For short journeys around cities, however, the *tuk-tuk* (motorized rickshaw) is your best and cheapest option. Just make sure the driver sets his meter— he may need to be reminded!

There are two types of taxi you can use, depending on where you want to go. Usually, black-and-yellow taxis operate within the state boundary, and tourist taxis, generally white, have an interstate or all-India license. Check this before hiring one if you are planning an interstate visit, otherwise you might be asked to pay a large amount of money at the border. It is also important to agree on a price before starting the journey as meters are often out of date or not working.

Car rental in India is unlike that in the West. There are very few self-drive companies, so you are limited to hiring a car and driver. This can be expensive if you hire a vehicle for a long period because the cost of car, fuel, and upkeep is quite high, even by Western standards. You can hire a self-drive motorcycle or scooter in some tourist and beach resorts, if you have exceptionally strong nerves.

Traveling at night by road between major cities, which may be hundreds of miles apart, is not recommended, as gangs of *dacoits* (robbers, from the word *daka,* to rob) are known to roam the countryside.

chapter seven

KEEPING HEALTHY

PREPARING TO GO

You'll need to check immunization requirements and other sensible precautions with your doctor before you go. Although there are no compulsory immunizations for a visit to India, the more adventurous you are, the more important it is to take precautions against hepatitis, typhoid, polio, tetanus, and malaria. Check any regional requirements, as meningitis is a seasonal risk in north India, and Japanese B encephalitis may be a risk in some areas. Take out a travel health insurance policy that will cover the cost of serious medical problems, and ensure that it covers the air fare home if medically necessary.

It is a good idea to take a small first-aid kit with you. Include disposable needles for injections, in case you ever require them in India. The "disposable" needles available in some pharmacies may have come from hospital waste bins and been only superficially cleaned. Treatments for diarrhea and dehydration are other essentials. If you need any regular medication, take enough to last the duration of your stay. Although most drugs are available over the counter in India, they may differ in composition between countries. If you need any medicines for local problems, pharmacists will help. The sun is strong in the Indian summer, and a high-strength sunblock cream (30 to 50) is essential.

Healthcare facilities vary from city to city, but if you need a doctor, go to a private hospital. Westerners will not find them expensive. Although many of the state hospitals are in a perilous state, the doctors are well qualified. You can get a list of recommended hospitals, and perhaps of some good private clinics, through your embassy.

INDIAN ATTITUDES TO HEALTH

As in all other aspects of Indian life, the belief in *karma* affects attitudes toward health. Suffering and illness are part of the *karmic* pattern of life. In poor communities, many people have no access to toilets, adequate washing facilities, or clean drinking water, and infectious and killer diseases such as tuberculosis, which have all but died out in the West, are rife. Death is encountered every day as so many people live, and die, on the street. You may have to step over dead bodies occasionally, and will on a daily basis pass open sewers, as well as piles of rubbish in the process of being picked over by children and animals.

People don't complain about illness as much as in the West. If you go to a doctor, you'll be expected to wait your turn patiently and calmly.

TRADITIONAL HEALTHCARE TREATMENTS

Because Indians see their health as interwoven with the whole picture—perhaps an illness is there to teach them something, or for some other reason—it follows that they are more open to holistic forms of medicine. Crucially, these are also usually cheaper than modern medicine.

The prevailing system of medicine in India is Ayurveda, an ancient holistic system with its own diagnostic principles and remedies, usually herbal. The root *Ayu* is Sanskrit for "life," while *Veda* implies "knowing." This sacred life science embraces the study of mind, body, behavior, environment, and religion. It has absorbed disciplines from many other cultures, but at its heart is the understanding that energy and matter are one. Doctors in India have often studied Ayurvedic medicine alongside their orthodox hospital training, and it is recognized in the West as an important complementary medical therapy. For those interested, there are many clinics specializing in teaching Ayurvedic medicine therapies. Homeopathic medicine is also widely available. If possible, locate practitioners who have had skills passed down through the generations.

Alexander the Great was Impressed!
The high quality of the indigenous Ayurvedic medicine so impressed Alexander the Great that he took physicians and practitioners back to Greece with him. This later returned to India with the Muslims as Unani, or Greco-Arabian, medicine, and still flourishes today.

PREVENTION IS BETTER THAN CURE
"Delhi belly" has become part of the English language, so it probably won't come as a surprise if you suffer a stomach upset. India is notorious for this kind of problem. Diarrhea is commonplace, and drinking contaminated water is nearly always the cause. You may use local water for washing, but water for drinking, or to be used for brushing your teeth, must be rigorously boiled and filtered, or else must come from a bottle. Check all bottle caps to make sure that the drink is the genuine

article and has not just been poured in by some enterprising soul around the corner.

Avoid raw foods such as salad and unpeeled fruit. Everything may look clean and fresh, but has probably been washed in tap water. As milk is not pasteurized, it must be boiled before drinking. Abundant flies and lack of hygiene, combined with skilled disguising of bad food, such as the copious use of spices on bad meat, mean that the safest option is to be vegetarian during your stay. Well-cooked vegetable and legume dishes, eggs, and freshly boiled rice are good and easily available.

Mosquitoes do not seem to bother the indigenous population unduly, but they are a problem in certain parts of India, and can carry malaria. The best way to avoid them is to stay in an air-conditioned hotel. All the pharmacies are well stocked with mosquito repellents.
You could also buy a mosquito net, or you could try the locally available All Out or Good Night. These are vials of nerve gas, for use in a small electric container, that keep the mosquitoes at bay. This seems to be quite harmless to human beings, for short periods.

Don't be tempted to touch stray dogs, or even those in private homes. Rabies is endemic in India.

If you are bitten, or even if the dog's saliva is on your skin, seek medical advice immediately.

SAFETY

India is not a menacing place, although caution should be exercised with regard to moving about after dark, as in many of the major cities of the world. Sexual harassment exists, and young Western women are seen as easy targets. Dress modestly and use your discretion. When you are out, keep your children with you. There isn't necessarily any danger, but in crowded places it will be easy for them to get lost.

Make sure your valuables—money, jewelry, passport, etc.—are locked up safely. It can be useful, for identification, to carry a copy of your passport with you.

Scams you may come across revolve around finding ways to part you from your money! Keep a close hold on your bag and money belt in crowded places, and watch out for pocket-sized pickpockets. Credit card fraud is a possibility, so guard your cards well at all times.

chapter eight

BUSINESS BRIEFING

The Indian way of doing business appears to be similar to that of the West, because the legal and business framework had its origins in the Raj. At another level, it is distinctly different, and a visitor hoping to do well in business in India must appreciate the differences. Make sure you know the management style of the organization you are dealing with, as there is a marked difference in leadership style between older and newer organizations. Many of the people you meet will have had an American or European education, often within India, and their behavior is strongly influenced by this.

That said, it is also wise to remember that these differences in no way diminish either the Indians' skill in negotiation, or their focus on profit. Their considerable commercial abilities are strengthened by family and trade alliances. Prime factors for getting ahead in India are connections, education, and hard work.

About 46 percent of the Indian population is illiterate, yet India, along with China, is seen as one of the most important markets in the world; indeed, it is developing into a major industrial power at an astonishing rate. The names of Tata, Oberoi, and Birla are internationally known. Tata and Oberoi have huge chains of luxury hotels all over India; Birla is an Indian industrialist.

The powerhouse of the economy is to be found in the northern states of Haryana, Punjab, Himachal Pradesh, Uttar Pradesh, Rajasthan, Jammu and Kashmir, together with the Union Territories of Delhi and Chandigarh. Punjab, principal home of the Sikhs, is known as India's breadbasket and has the highest per capita income.

Business hours are usually 9:30 a.m. to 5:30 p.m., Monday to Friday. Government offices are open 10:00 a.m. to 5.00 p.m., Monday to Saturday, closing from 1:00 p.m. to 2:00 p.m. for lunch. They also close on the second Saturday of each month. Shops usually close in the afternoon from 1:00 p.m. to 4:00 p.m., but stay open till 9:00 p.m.

CORE BUSINESS ATTITUDES

Right from the start, it is important to recognize that all general statements about business attitudes and values must be modified by your experience of the corporation or company you are dealing with, and also by the background of the individual. A high-tech firm in Bangalore run by a Harvard

MBA-educated Indian may be very different from a family business in Mumbai (Bombay) run by someone who has not had overseas business experience. Nevertheless, corporate culture is, to a degree, anchored in national culture, and it is worth being aware of basic attitudes and values.

A Relationship-Based Culture

Business success depends on building the right relationship with your business partners and clients. This can take time, and you should not try to hurry it. Friendship and kinship are often more important than expertise, but titles and diplomas are prized. Westerners tend to believe in *carpe diem,* or seizing the opportunity. Indians tend to trust in the wheel of life, believing that opportunities not grasped now will come again later, although perhaps not in the same form. Humility is seen as a virtue.

The Importance of *Karma*

A key Indian attitude is a strong belief in *karma.* As well as predestination and reincarnation, the Indians believe in cycles: "What goes around, comes around." Success and failure are often attributed to environmental factors. If a deal or transaction is completed, it is due to *karma.* If it isn't, it is also *karma.* Allied with this is a considerable degree of superstition. A meeting or contract signing may be arranged for a day that is astrologically auspicious rather than convenient. This can cause delay and frustration if you are not aware of what is going on in the minds of those you're dealing with.

Respect for Elders

A very important aspect of business is showing deference to elders, which means politeness, respect when addressing them personally, and not ignoring them. With this goes a degree of warmth in business dealings that in no way belies the strength of the profit motive or firmness and acuity in negotiation.

Experiment and Eloquence

The Indians are good risk takers, and admire creative and experimental business solutions. They also admire eloquence (Indian English is flowery and verbose) and applaud ideas presented with flair and enthusiasm. The objective is success in business (the honor of the family or the trade groups demands it), but failure may be attributed to bad *karma,* and therefore not seen as personal failure. You will also find that Indians are not inhibited in the expression of joy or sadness, even in business situations.

Saving Face

Indians believe that personal reputations must be upheld, and will go to some lengths not to criticize others or state unpalatable truths. This means that honesty is essentially relative. People would rather tell you a lie than upset you or disagree with you. For your part, be careful to nurture your good relationships. It is important to stress the exact nature of the information you need, in order to elicit the right responses. Always treat your Indian colleagues with respect, and never criticize or correct them in front of others. Indians are very sensitive to criticism, and also, understandably, don't respond well if Westerners are arrogant or patronizing toward them.

At the end of a conference in Mumbai (Bombay), the Indian delegates made a presentation to the main speaker, who was British. It was a highly decorated sculpture of the elephant god Ganesh. The speaker opened the present in front of the delegates and was visibly less than impressed. Not recognizing the god, he thanked the delegates for this "bright, almost garish ornament," and said that it would look good in his conservatory at home. He also made a passing joke about its value as a bird scarer. This was clumsy by any standards, but his Indian hosts felt that both they and he had lost face by his failure to appreciate a ritual object offered as thanks, and the conference ended on a less agreeable note.

THE BUSINESS CULTURE

The business community is closely knit and its survival is centered on family welfare. More than 70 percent of the hundred largest corporations and 99.9 percent of all enterprises in India are either owned or controlled by families. The story goes that when a certain merchant belonging to the Agarwal business community became insolvent, 99,999 businesses donated one rupee and one brick to him so that he could restart his business and rebuild his house!

There are twenty-two stock exchanges and, it is often stated, 7,000 quoted companies, of which perhaps just over 1,000 are active, and over 25 million shareholders. Shares are available on every street corner in practically every kind of enterprise. Long lines can be seen during the lunch break, when the workers rush to get their share of the latest stock offering.

Different regional centers have developed key industries. Bangalore is known as the "silicon valley" of India, for instance, and Mumbai (Bombay) heads the film and media industries.

Since July 1991, India's economic isolation, which had been one of the cornerstones of her postindependence policy, has been replaced by liberalization and economic reforms. Impressive changes are being stimulated with many import restrictions abolished and tariff barriers being notably reduced. The rupee is fully convertible for purposes of trade, and direct financial investment is now permitted. The financial industry has been deregulated as regards mutual funds.

Industrialists petitioning for new licenses for expansion or for joint ventures with foreign partners are finding that their applications are now processed with greater ease. There is also no shortage of individuals and organizations claiming to have the knowledge and expertise to represent you in India. It is worth remembering that quality control is new to India, and occasionally there is a great difference in the samples shown to win an order and the goods that are eventually shipped.

Watch Out for Unsolicited Letters
Western firms are now inundated by unsolicited letters from Indians wanting to become their agents. As some of them might be unscrupulous, it is worth researching them thoroughly.

In an effort to woo back Indians who left as part of the massive brain drain, and get them to reinvest in India, the government has instigated a special scheme. Indians abroad, whether they are Indian or foreign nationals (as long as their parents were born in India), have a special status of Non-Resident

Indian, or NRI. They, their spouses, and their children enjoy all the privileges of an Indian national except voting rights. They are all described as "having Indian origins," even if their spouse happens to be American or English.

Using English

English is the common language of business all over India. Understanding it, however, can be a different matter, and this can cause significant problems. If you don't understand what an Indian is saying to you, just politely ask him or her to repeat it, and prompt tactfully if necessary. Don't make the mistake of assuming that they are unintelligent. Take the trouble to listen carefully to what is being said.

Business cards printed in English are extensively used. Qualifications in India are worn on the sleeve and certainly flaunted on a business card. Be sure to have all your qualifications clearly listed after your name.

Formality and Flexibility

Business is quite formal. For a man, business suit and tie are appropriate for meetings. In general office environments, more informal clothing is acceptable. Indian businessmen normally wear Western clothes, and remove ties and jackets in excessive heat.

Women should wear smart Western clothes, and avoid leather products such as bags, belts, and purses, so as not to offend Hindu sensibilities. Very often, you'll notice that Indian women working in institutions such as banks wear a uniform. Affluent Indian women are very fashion-conscious and love to dress up, so take something suitable to wear for evening functions.

All decisions are made at the top of the company, so it makes sense to approach an organization at this level. Although you must deal with and show proper respect to the senior man, quite often the middle manager will be the most useful informant.

Make appointments well in advance, but be prepared to be flexible. Accept that everything takes time. Business is not conducted on religious holidays, which are numerous and vary between the regions.

WOMEN IN BUSINESS

While it is important to recognize that women have occupied top positions in Indian society, and you may come across women in positions of seniority in business and administration, Indian society is quite chauvinistic in Western terms. A woman should be aware that inviting a male colleague to her hotel room for a business meeting is quite likely to be misunderstood by the local community, and she will be treated accordingly. It is perfectly acceptable to invite a man to eat with you, but be aware that he may try to pay.

Indian men prefer shy, self-effacing women, and are generally not accustomed to dealing with women in authority. They may feel awkward dealing with senior foreign businesswomen. Being warm, friendly, and natural should help to ease the situation.

BUSINESS COMMUNICATIONS

India is a relationship-based culture, and so your initial contact will often be made through common business associates. Oral agreements are very important in India, and contracts are often considered as statements of intent that can be modified. It is a good idea to maintain multiple channels of communication.

Telephone answering machines are seen as impersonal and therefore may not elicit a response; mobile telephones are the key communication medium here.

You can't build business relationships on written communication only, but the Indians like a formal approach in writing. In such an approach, adopt a formal, eloquent style. Use detailed letters to agree on business terms, although you should be prepared for your partners to ask for agreements to be modified. However, bear in mind that the Indian postal service is slow, and faxes are often not treated as urgent. E-mail is being rapidly adopted, and is the best way to reach someone quickly.

The Indian people are generally warm and responsive, and show an interest in your personal life. They are generally better speakers than listeners, and body language, tone of voice, and inflection are important. Indian businesspeople adopt a formal style of speech, and foreign businesspeople should follow their lead. Don't boast about your achievements, although older people may remind you of their educational qualifications, which are a source of pride.

Politeness, praise, and respect are important and, eager not to cause offense, people generally "edit" their thoughts. You need to develop a tolerance for ambiguity in conversation.

Reflecting their collectivist culture, the Indians use "we" rather than "I"; interruption is common. An outright "no" is considered harsh, but evasive refusals are polite and accepted. Vagueness from an Indian usually means "no," and "I'll try" is an acceptable form of refusal.

You need to take care not to leave any issues unsettled, but be aware that Indians don't like to be hurried. In order not to embarrass or humiliate people, try not to be confrontational or peremptory in communications.

PRESENTATIONS

You may find the tradition of presentation in India frustrating. The Indians are educated to give the reasons for a decision or a point before making the point itself. You may hear yourself listening to a long preamble and wondering if there is any point to it at all. There is, but it will be stated at the end, not at the beginning as we are used to hearing it. On the one hand, many Indians are fond of flowery language and tend to be verbose. On the other, those who have had a Western education will get to the point quickly.

Make sure you show an interest in the speaker's vision and ideas, and a willingness to be persuaded to a point of view. Show that you appreciate eloquent speech and elaborate description.

If you are making the presentation, bear in mind that the Indian attention span is moderate: about forty-five minutes is the optimum presentation length. It is important to display your education, expertise, and experience in giving presentations to Indians, while maintaining strong eye contact and expressive body language. Repeat your key points several times and make sure you bring out your Indian audience's perspective or ask for their point of view. Show warmth, sympathy, commitment, and enthusiasm. An Indian audience likes to give feedback, so you need to allow time for this, and do not ignore suggestions. Indicate at what point you will be ready to accept questions.

MEETINGS AND NEGOTIATIONS

The main objective of meetings is to discuss matters and examine issues in detail, but you should also use them to establish good personal relationships. Seating is hierarchical, and the meetings will be structured, although agendas are not strictly adhered to. Be punctual, though others may be late.

Negotiations often involve large groups of people. Aims may be revealed, but objectives may not be discussed until later. Indians are usually flexible, patient negotiators, although they often use personalized and sometimes emotional arguments. You need to show a willingness to compromise, in the interest of good long-term relations.

An interesting cultural mismatch occurred in a proposed joint venture between an Indian and a U.S. firm. The chairman of the Indian company was on hand to welcome his American colleagues. The American company sent a vice-president and four people for a two-day negotiation, and asked in advance for the Indians' proposed organization chart showing the key positions in the new joint venture. They never received it. In the course of the two-day discussions the Americans asked again for the proposed organization chart. The Indians responded, "Tell us what you want!" The Americans then proceeded to negotiate. The Indians smiled and said little. When the Americans returned home they received a proposed organization chart from their Indian colleagues. In it, Indians held most of the top positions.

Furious, the Americans accused their Indian counterparts of duplicity. "Why didn't you tell us while we were there?" they fumed. "Why did we go all that way for nothing?" The Indian reply was revealing. "We were not going to fight with you while you were guests in our country," they said. "We wanted to be hospitable!"

Encourage rapport by being warm, friendly, and courteous. A little time spent asking after friends and family will help to build relationships. Be ready to learn from your Indian colleagues, and don't forget to show respect for seniority. As with everything in India, take your time, and don't be tempted to rush people into decisions.

Emphasize your common aims, rely on good relationships to get things done, and don't give up when faced with apathy or setbacks. In meetings and negotiations, you need to be able to tolerate ambiguity, and don't forget that people will often tell you what they think you want to hear. Don't assume that smiling faces mean acceptance.

DECISION-MAKING

Since India is a moderately collectivist culture, individual decisions must be in harmony with the individual's family, group, and social structure. The organizational structure, however, is vertical, and the responsibility for decision-making tends to rest with a small group whose authority is often based on wealth and family background. Staff respect authority, although they will protest against perceived injustice.

As with everything in India, decisions are arrived at slowly. There is no point in trying to impose strict deadlines. Show consideration by allowing plenty of time for discussion so that people can air their views, which they will often do heatedly; Indians appeal to people's emotions in order to persuade them.

Show that you are willing to share the risk in a proposed venture, and respect others' views. Remember that the Indian people are generally too polite to say "no" outright.

CORRUPTION IS RELATIVE

No book on India would be complete without some mention of corruption. For a society based on relationships, a reward for personal services is not necessarily regarded as corrupt. This shades into the practice of offering inducements in advance. Every contract can be fiddled, any privilege bought, every examination wangled. This practice is so widespread that it pervades every stratum in society, and is simply accepted as a fact of life. It might be better described as a "surcharge," or "an Indian custom." To accommodate it, a "number two" bank account is common.

Businessmen regularly pay huge sums of money to ministers and bureaucrats, first to expedite some application form or other, and then to prevent its obstruction. The speed with which something is achieved has often been described as "how big a smile you put on the face" of the relevant official. It is best to be guided by your business partner if you are planning to do business in India.

WINING AND DINING

Entertaining is an important part of doing business in India, not least because it helps to build relationships and to allow you to ask those all-important personal questions about

friends and family. The divide between home and work is more fluid than in the West, and entertaining is quite often done at home. If you're going out, entertainment for middle-class Indians centers on the traditional clubs, such as the Bombay Club, or the Mumbai

Cricket Club, and so on, which contain sports facilities, bars, restaurants, and meeting-rooms. Some of these have strict dress codes; for instance, in the Bangalore Club men are not allowed in the lounges without long trousers and a tie. On formal occasions, suits are obligatory.

Refreshments such as tea and cakes accompany business. Invitations to drinks and snacks are common, and on the whole business lunches are preferred to dinners. Arriving fifteen to thirty minutes after the appointed time is common practice. People tend to drink water (only from sealed bottles), soft drinks, or beer with their food.

Although as a foreigner your differences will be allowed for, always remember to wash your hands both before and after a meal, and, if using your fingers, eat only with the right hand. It is polite to ask before you smoke.

Most Indian meals are vegetarian, with a little meat on the side; remember that Hindus don't eat beef and Muslims don't eat pork. Thank your hosts for the meal, but it is more important to show appreciation by inviting them back.

Be a Good Guest

An American businessman living in Bangalore was invited to a Hindu wedding. At a traditional wedding, you sit on the floor, the meal is served on banana leaves, and you eat with your fingers. The groom was concerned about how the businessman would respond, and offered to have a place set for him at the table, with a plate and cutlery; but the businessman told him to not to worry, that he wanted to be treated like everyone else. Although everyone noticed he made a thorough mess of eating, they really appreciated his efforts.

ALL THE TIME IN THE WORLD

Time-keeping is not an Indian strength. Your punctuality will be expected, but don't assume that the Indians will be on time. Delays are normal and to be expected, so be prepared to be kept waiting for appointments. It is a standing joke that IST (Indian Standard Time) really stands for Indian Stretchable Time. Westerners in India have difficulty in understanding this fluidity in relation to time; patience is key. If you try to rush things, you will risk offending your hosts and you won't get anywhere.

BUREAUCRACY

Bureaucracy is rife in India. People seem to have a passion for paper, documents, and ledgers. Parts of India are very high-tech, but not everyone is computer literate and old systems of form-filling are very much in operation. In many businesses, expect to fill out all forms in triplicate. Ask your Indian colleagues to show you creative solutions to cut through the paperwork. Surprisingly, attitudes toward officialdom outside the bureaucratic system are fairly relaxed.

Red Tape

Requirements for travel documents need to be checked prior to departure, as these can often change. You will need to get double or triple re-entry visas if traveling in and out of India. If your stay in India is going to take you beyond the date of issue, a three-month extension is routinely given on the production of four passport photographs. If you stay longer than three months, you will need to hand in an income tax clearance certificate upon departure. This is available from the main tax offices. You will also require permits if you want to visit restricted areas, such as Sikkim. Extensions and permits are both available from Foreigners' Registration Offices or from the Superintendent of Police at District Headquarters.

Services

With 150,000 post offices, India has the largest postal network in the world. Efficiency, however, is another matter. It can sometimes take two weeks for a letter to travel

thirty miles (forty-eight kilometers). As letters going to foreign countries have to have *tikets*, or stamps that are quite expensive by Indian standards, it is not unusual for these to disappear from the envelopes before they can be postmarked. To avoid this, either have stamps stuck on and then "defaced" at the post office, or, better still, take letters to a main post office, where they will be franked for the right amount of money. If you need to send a letter urgently, opt for international couriers, found in all the major cities.

chapter nine

COMMUNICATING

THE LANGUAGES OF INDIA

The official language of India is Hindi, but fourteen major and three hundred minor languages are also spoken, and there are an estimated 874 regional dialects. Other languages you may hear are Urdu, the court language left by the Persians and still used by the Muslims; Punjabi, spoken by the Sikhs; and Gujarati, spoken by Parsis and Hindus. Gujarati and Marathi are regional languages.

Hindi is a mixture of words derived from Sanskrit and Urdu, and is spoken in the north. The Dravidians, with seven major and many minor languages, were already in southern India when the Aryans brought Sanskrit to India's shores. These languages, including Tamil, Kannada, and Malayalam, are spoken by over 110 million people.

In the nineteenth century, English became the medium of higher education, the language of administration, and the lingua franca of the educated population. But you might find it difficult to understand, even among the educated classes, whose own understanding may well be better than their spoken English. There are huge variations in dialect and pronunciation, and Indian English differs in some grammatical and lexical aspects from "International English." If you don't understand what is being said to you, politely and slowly ask your interlocutor to repeat it.

The government had hoped that making Hindi the national language would produce a national identity, but the impact of the British in India is still felt. The southern Indians don't understand Hindi, and generally rely on English to communicate with northern Indians. Indeed, English is often referred to as the only language common to all Indians.

CONVERSATION

Small talk is part of the Indian way of life. As we have seen, people will ask quite personal questions about your salary, home, job, family, marriage, and so on, which can be embarrassing for some foreigners. The Indians have no problems in expressing emotion either, although you should be careful with directness: "no" is considered harsh, for instance.

Western humor may not be fully understood, but charm and laughter are appreciated. The same goes for flattery and compliments, which the Indians use liberally to put people at ease. Group harmony is an important aspect to bear in mind when you are communicating with the Indians. Like anywhere else in the world, a smile and readiness to respond will always pave the way to better communication and good relations.

Telling You What You Want to Hear

It is important to realize that people in India may say what they think you want to hear, rather than tell you the objective truth. Bear this in mind when asking questions. "Is the temple this way?" will almost invariably be answered with "yes." Frame your questions carefully to elicit the correct response, such as "Which way is the temple?" However, "I don't know" doesn't enter into the Indian vocabulary very frequently. A direction will be given, with assurances, even if the person has no idea where the temple is.

The Indians value eloquence, which can lead to long speeches, spoken with passion. Likewise in conversation they will usually present reasons first and give conclusions afterward, which may leave you lost halfway through, and wondering what point they're trying to make.

Respect for education and formality means use of surnames and titles, particularly with older people, so don't use first names unless they suggest it. With the younger generation, however, first names are more common. Indians often use "Sir" and "Madam" to attract attention.

BODY LANGUAGE

Body language in India is subtle but important. Nodding the head as in the West means "yes," and shaking the head from side to side is "no." However, the most common, characteristic, and striking gesture in India is a distinctive, rotational movement of the head. This can have several meanings. With a smile it might mean agreement, or "Okay, I understand," or it could be "maybe." More often than not, it is "I couldn't care less!" Westerners find it very catching, and often involuntarily imitate it. A more vigorous head tilt can mean either excitement or an angry rebuttal.

Traditionally, the head and the ears are sacred in Indian culture. Never pat a child on the head, which is seen as the seat of the soul, and feet or shoes should not touch anyone else as they are considered unclean—and probably are! Apologize immediately if this happens.

Some Do's and Don'ts

- Indians point with a jerk of the chin. Never point with your finger; this is considered rude.
- Indians beckon with palm down and fingers pulling inward.
- Whistling and winking are considered impolite.
- Grasping your own ears signifies repentance or sincerity.

CONCLUSION

India is a land of contrasts and diversity. Be prepared for an assault on your senses, and a challenge to your preconceptions. Above all, however, it is the warmth, vitality, humor, and energy of the Indian people that leave the most lasting impression.

"After six-and-a-half months in India, I couldn't wait to leave. Strange now that it's the first place I would return to. Then again, that's how it is with India. It is an intense place; wonderful and exotic and depressing and frustrating and mind-blowing. Sometimes all at the same time. If you have endurance, patience, a flair for adventure, and a desire for the unexpected, there are few places you will love more than India."

Mark Elliott, working traveler

Further Reading

There is a vast range of books on every conceivable aspect of India. Here are a few titles to start with.

Abram, David, et al. *The Rough Guide to India.*
London: Rough Guides, 2001.

Kingsland, Venika. *Simple Guide to Hinduism.*
Folkestone, Kent: Global Books, 1999.

Lewis, Richard D. *When Cultures Collide: Managing Successfully Across Cultures.* London: Nicholas Brealey Publishing, 1999.

O'Reilly, James P., and Larry Habegger (eds.). *India.*
San Francisco, California: Travelers' Tales, 1995.

Singh, Sarina, et al. *Lonely Planet: India.*
Melbourne/Oakland/London/Paris: Lonely Planet Publications, 2000.

Tammita-Delgoda, SinhaRaja. *A Traveller's History of India.*
Moreton-in-Marsh, Gloucestershire: Windrush Press, 1994;
Northampton, Mass.: 1994; London: Cassell, 2002.

Complete Hindi. New York: Living Language, 2006/7

culture smart! **india**

Index